ISABEL BEST

QUEENS OF PAIN

LEGENDS & REBELS OF CYCLING

Rapha.

Queens of Pain: Legends and Rebels of Cycling
© Isabel Best, 2018

Isabel Best has asserted his right under the Copyright, Designs and Patents Act, 1988, to be identified as the Author of this work. All rights reserved. No part of this publication may be reproduced or transmitted in any form or by any means, electronic or mechanical, including photocopying, recording, or any information storage or retrieval system, without prior permission in writing from the publishers. No responsibility for loss caused to any individual or organisation acting on or refraining from action as a result of the material in this publication can be accepted by Rapha, Rapha Editions, Bluetrain Publishing Ltd. or the author.

All images © as listed on page 240

First published in 2018
by Rapha Racing Ltd.
Imperial Works, 18 Tileyard, London, N7 9AH

Rapha founder and CEO: Simon Mottram
Publishing director: Daniel Blumire
Executive publishers: Sarah Clark
and Charlie Pym
Rapha design director: Jack Saunders
Rapha Editions liaison: Emma Wallace

Published for Rapha Editions,
in arrangement with
Bluetrain Publishing Ltd.
bluetrainpublishing.com

Editor: Taz Darling
Publishing editor: Guy Andrews
Art direction: Bluetrain
Copy editor: Anya Hayes
Image retouching: Linda Duong
Book design: Melanie Mues,
Mues Design London
muesdesign.com

Printed and bound by SYL, Barcelona, Spain

ISBN 978-1-912164-05-9

All rights reserved.

RAPHA.CC

For my mother and her seven granddaughters

ISABEL BEST

QUEENS OF PAIN

LEGENDS & REBELS OF CYCLING

CONTENTS

Introduction 6

Tillie Anderson 10
Hélène Dutrieux 24
Alfonsina Strada 34
Evelyn Hamilton 42
Marguerite Wilson 52

The Australians: 66
Doreen Middleton
Billie Samuel
Joyce Barry
Valda Unthank
Pat Hawkins

Eileen Sheridan 82
Lyli Herse 94
Millie Robinson 110
Elsy Jacobs 122
Beryl Burton 130
Yvonne Reynders 142

Lubow Kotchetova 154
Audrey McElmury 170
The Hage Sisters 180
Connie Carpenter-Phinney 190
Marianne Martin 200
Maria Canins 212
Jeannie Longo 220
Inga Thompson 230

Credits 239

INTRODUCTION

There's a certain classic photograph of a racing cyclist from the 1920s. It is raining and the rider wears a mud-caked woollen jersey and shorts. A thousand yard stare issues from a face worn with the indescribable effort of a race just completed. It has obviously been a filthy day. The perfect day for a *flahute* – a leathery tough sort in the mould of Lucien Buysse, who won the 1926 Tour de France thanks to an epic Pyreneen ride in apocalyptic weather. Our picture was taken in 1926 though it is not of Buysse but of a woman, the French Champion Suzanne Hudry. But that's probably all we'll ever know of her. Her name doesn't appear in any history books. She isn't on any official lists of French champions. I haven't found her in any newspaper or magazine archives, and the championship race she won is a mystery, since (as far as the French Cycling Federation is concerned) there were no national championships for women before 1951. If it wasn't for this photograph, Suzanne Hudry wouldn't exist. Everything that was painfully real to her at the time, the training hours she would have had to fit around her low-status, low-paid job, her 'men's' racing bike that would have cost a month's wages or more, the race itself and all her worthy adversaries – all this has been forgotten. Yet her picture is evidence that women were racing – seriously – in France in the 1920s.

> 'Is there really such a thing, women's cycling?'
> —Georges Pompidou at the Salon du Cyclisme in 1972

In the process of writing this book I have frequently felt like a detective, hunting for clues. Sometimes the trail goes cold. At other times I've met eloquent witnesses, watched beguiling clips of newsreel or stumbled across treasure troves of archive material. What I have discovered is that there have always been women like Suzanne Hudry, and that they have been giving it their all since bike racing was invented.

I'm not talking about novelty races where the ladies 'got to have a go', but proper blood-and-guts racing, for serious money, often drawing in audiences of thousands, sometimes generating detailed commentary and press reports – and at one point even provoking a riot. And that was in 1896, before the Tour de France had even begun.

Women's racing gets such scant mention in cycling literature you'd be forgiven for thinking it had no history. How many people know, for example, that there was a women's Tour de France between 1984 and 1989? Who knew that the women rode the same roads and on the same days as the men? Where is the folklore about the epic rivalry played out between two riders who *should* be up there in the Pantheon of the greats: Maria Canins and Jeannie Longo?

Suzanne Hudry, 1926. French national champion © BtA

There are official histories, and there are unofficial histories. If you believe the official histories, women's world record attempts only began in 1955. Women's international road racing began in 1958 and it only became suitable for Olympic inclusion in 1984. Time trials were only introduced to the world championships in 1994 and to the Olympics in 1996. Thirty years too late for Beryl Burton, 40 years too late for Eileen Sheridan, 60 years too late for Marguerite Wilson and Valda Unthank, 70 years too late for Alfonsina Strada and a 100 years overdue for Tillie Anderson – riders who almost certainly could have added TT gold to their palmarès.

What makes a champion? At what point does a rider become 'great' if they have all the qualities, but not the stage on which to express their brilliance? You can't ride like Fausto Coppi if your race only goes round a housing estate. The women in this book demonstrated their athletic prowess by dominating the races that were allowed them, or riding 1,000 miles continuously in terrible weather to set point to point records. They trained at 5am before going to work, or at 8pm after their children were in bed. They broke men's records, rode through blizzards and had all the race cunning of a veteran *directeur sportif*.

They would ride for 100 miles to take part in a 10-mile time-trial and work 12-hour days, six days a week, travel on night trains so they could race on Sundays, then get the sleeper back for work on Monday morning. They set up their own clubs and races. They paid their own travel costs for the privilege of representing their country at international races. They pretended to be men so they could train on their local velodromes. They rode with broken collarbones or with their hands strapped to their handlebars after crashes. For their efforts, they were rewarded with pepper grinders, silk stockings, ironing boards, and, if they got really lucky, a year's supply of laundry detergent.

This book finishes in the early 1990s, when women's cycling finally became a professional sport to which (some) riders were able to dedicate their careers, not just weekends and holidays. However if there is a lesson to be drawn from these pages it is that women will get on their bikes and rise to the opportunities available to them. Parity with men's racing remains a distant goal but there will be no shortage of available heroines the closer it gets.

Isabel Best

The first womens' world road race. Reims circuit, France, 1958.
© Presse Sports/Offside

TILLIE ANDERSON

'Tillie the Terrible Swede'

In 1939, a 64-year-old lady drove 650 miles from Minnesota to the Chicago suburb of Northbrook, stopping only for petrol, in order to get to a party to which she hadn't been invited.

At the Sportsmans' Golf Club, the stag reunion of 19th–century racing cyclists had already been in flow for a good two hours when her car crunched its way up the gravelled drive. A local reporter was at the party, where Frank Wing of Ottawa, 'was exhibiting perhaps the most complete set of scrapbooks on old time bike riding in existence,' Ald. James Bowler [25th] was, 'all set to tell of his Six-day bike riding days', J.P. "Pye" Bliss, the world champion at the mile in 1893, 1894 and 1895, 'had been demonstrating his technique,' and Edward Kreutzinger 'was showing his collection of 450 bicycle name plates.' But all that, we learn, 'was before Tillie came.' Tillie Shoberg stepped out of her car, adjusted her hat, smoothed down her skirt and walked confidently in, never mind the fact that 'no reservation had been made for her at dinner.'

The assembled gentlemen looked up in surprise.

'But Mrs Shoberg had only to mention her maiden name to get the attention of the 75 cyclists assembled. A hush fell over the old timers as, one by one, they stepped forward to shake her hand and tell her how well she looked "after all these years".'

Basking in their admiration, 'She told of winning 123 races out of 129 in 1895, her big year. She boasted of having done the half-mile in 52 seconds [the best Pye Bliss ever did was 1:47 for the mile]. But what thrilled Tillie most was the realization that she was one of the few at the reunion who had kept her figure.'

Tillie Anderson had every right to feel pleased with herself after all these years, and not just about keeping trim. She had been the champion of champions. She had crested a wave of immensely talented young women who, in the space of seven years, had drawn audiences in their thousands and made headlines across the United States. Their rivalries were the subject of long and detailed analysis in the press, but most of all it was their record-breaking prowess, their bravado and their speed, that held audiences enthralled.

Publicity shot for Chicago bike manufacturer Thistle. © Alice Olson Roepke Collection

The riders were mostly immigrants who perfectly symbolised the verve of America poised on the brink of the 20th century, where there were no limiting horizons, where anyone with a bit of pluck and imagination could have a go at making it, the only condition being that you did it the best.

They raced on tiny, temporary wooden velodromes set up in public meeting halls, featuring as many as 16 or 21 laps to the mile, which people took to calling saucers, or sugar bowls. The banking was steep – sometimes approaching 45° – and the curves so tight, there was no question of riding at anything less than top speed if a rider wanted to keep control of her bike. As they whirled round the vortex their bodies seemed to hang horizontally in the air.

On occasion, a rider went too high up the banking and flew off into the audience. Riders also had to pay attention not to dash their heads against the bridge that allowed spectators access to the centre of the track. Other hazards included the tacks boys sometimes scattered in the hope of provoking punctures and crashes. A rider who crashed was given a certain number of laps – usually amounted to less than a minute – to get back into the race without losing her position. Their races were in the main Six-day events featuring three hours of racing a day. Riding in teams, they would compete through the afternoon and into the night, collaborating to beat the other group yet also vying for individual glory with the aim of covering the greatest distances and breaking new speed and distance records.

Just as in a modern stage race on the road, much could happen in the course of a week – a rider might be plagued with bad luck and injuries, drop behind by many laps and consider retiring, and then two days later bounce back into contention. The suspense would build into a crescendo so that by the end of the week, race organisers were turning people away at the door. On one occasion, the feverish excitement even triggered a riot when Tillie's great rival, Dottie Farnsworth, decided to pull out of the final day of a race in Minneapolis in 1896. A crowd of 5,000 fans, who had paid double the usual admission for the last day, 'grew wild,' the Saint Paul Globe reported. 'The spectators broke through the railing and made the track impassable,' and when the police turned up, 'a lively hand-to-hand fight was soon going on between the officers and the angry mob... clubs had to be used and in some instances revolvers were flourished. Several of the officers were struck by flying rocks.'

Newspapers devoted many column inches to these races, even without riots. In this new era, where there were still no 'norms' and where each detail was being invented, journalists reported on everything with the zest and increasingly savvy analysis of modern sports correspondents. They tracked average speeds, distances notched and records broken, but also riders' individual strengths and styles of riding, their bravery, bravado and spats. The great champions became celebrities who criss-crossed the US drawing huge crowds wherever they went. They had nicknames like 'Red Bird,' 'White Cyclone' or 'Beauty.' The most famous of all were Tillie Anderson, Lizzie Glaw, Dottie Farnsworth, Helen Baldwin and May Allen, who collectively became known as 'The Big Five.' And then, as quickly as women's racing had arrived, it disappeared. Some women tried racing cars or motorcycles, or got into the stunt business. Others got married or found other jobs. Mostly, they just disappeared from the public eye.

> When these women died, their stories went with them.

Roger Gilles, who uncovers this scene in his eye-opening and meticulously researched book, *Women On The Move: The Forgotten Era Of Women's Bicycle Racing,* tried contacting the descendants of many of these riders. To his surprise, he was often the first to tell them about their remarkable grandmothers and great grandmothers. Either the riders hadn't kept memorabilia or it had all been lost. They never talked about their past triumphs. Since The League of American Wheelmen refused to recognize their races, there is no official record of their results, either. When these women died, their stories went with them. Tillie Anderson, however, was the exception.

In the woods of Northern Minnesota there is a wood cabin built in the 1920s: Tillie's holiday home, paid for with her race winnings. It has a simple, spartan charm; the sort of place you fantasise about escaping to, with a few novels and a fishing rod for company. Nothing has changed. Hung up above the window is one of her racing bikes. The crockery and cutlery in the kitchen is all hers. The cabin belongs to her great niece now, who has kept everything in loving memory of a family legend, a woman who got on with things and didn't suffer fools, but was also devoted to her nephews and nieces. Inside there are the two trunks Tillie travelled across America with. They are stuffed with a treasure trove of cuttings books, medals, a racing jersey or two, Tillie's handwritten notes on her competitors, score cards from races, rivals' signed photographs and other memorabilia.

Tillie Anderson was born in Sweden in 1875 and grew up on a farm, the fourth of five children. She worked on neighbouring farms to bring in extra money to support her mother. Brought up in the strict Lutheran tradition, she never shirked pulling her weight.

She arrived in America in 1891 when she was 16 years old. She had travelled with her younger brother August. They joined their older sister Hanna who had gone out two years previously and was working in Chicago as a seamstress. Her mother and remaining two siblings came out the following year.

One can only imagine how 1890s Chicago must have appeared to a young woman from the Swedish countryside, with its wind-funnelling streets laid out in a gigantic grid and its mix of ever-growing skyscrapers with huge glass windows, palatial villas, steel mills and slums. A polyglot city, thrusting upwards and outwards, that had doubled its population in just ten years to become one of the biggest in the world, where two fifths of the population had converged from abroad.

What Tillie noticed most of all was the droves of independent, unchaperoned young women wheeling round the city on the diamond-framed safety bicycles that were taking Chicago by storm. Between 1890 and 1896, the number of local bicycle manufacturers increased from 4 to 25, and by 1897 an estimated 1 in 5 Chicagoans rode. Whatever it took, Tillie was going to have one of these bikes, too. It took her two years of working, in a laundry during the day and as a seamstress by night, before she could afford her very own; the cheapest she could buy, weighing over 40 pounds, acquired in the summer of 1894 when she was 19. She would get up before 5am to ride 20 to 40 miles before work, and in the evenings and at weekends she would explore the city and its outskirts.

There was no shortage of other riders to measure herself up against, and she quickly saw she could hold her own among the city's 'scorchers' – the young bloods who loved to speed. The following year she took part in her first 'century' along the famous Elgin–Aurora route West of Chicago. The women's record stood at 7 hours and 15 minutes. Tillie reduced it to 6 hours and 57 minutes. Between June and October she rode a further seven centuries, but there were other ambitious riders including Lizzie Glaw, a girl of German origin, who rode the century course 36 times that year. Tillie managed to get the record down to 6 hours and 52 minutes.

She made another important discovery in church, that of a handsome young chap of Swedish origin like herself, called J. Philip Shoberg, who, better still, was a respected racing cyclist. They soon fell in love, and Philip became Tillie's coach and guide in all matters cycling. He got her training seriously, 'I was very weak when I began, but now I never suffer from pains and aches as most women do,' she later said. 'I think it is a delightful sport and the best possible exercise, though I regularly practice club-swinging, dumb-bell lifting, a little boxing, take lots of outdoor exercise, and look after my health as best I can.'

Tillie took part in her first Six-day race in January 1896, in Chicago. The race promoter was a Frenchman, H.O. Messier, who had already put on a wildly successful Six-day race in Minneapolis over Christmas.

Tillie was taken on as a wild card, on the basis of her good century times, and the fact that she was a local girl who might therefore appeal to the crowd.

Previous pages: Tillie wrote of herself as, 'a natural blond very fair, falsely accused of being a peroxide blond, rode with ease.' © Alice Olson Roepke Collection

But on the first day of trying out the track, a week before the race, Tillie crashed five times. The coach, 'Dad' Moulton, whom Messier had brought on board to help the girls, took Philip to one side and suggested that she that she leave. Philip pleaded with him to let her stay. Tillie not only stopped crashing, but improved with each day of practice, so that by the end of the week she was as confident as her more experienced rivals. She went on to win the entire Six-day race.

This marked the start of her extraordinary career. That year she took part in eight Six-day races and won all but one. She also took part in 16 'match races' out of which she won 14. She became a celebrity overnight.

The following year – 1897 – she rode 30 races and won 28. Travelling with her bike and a trunk, she got on trains that crossed the length and breadth of the USA, as far afield as Ohio, Louisiana and Montana. Most of her destinations read like a roll-call of America's great industrial cities: Cleveland, Detroit, Minneapolis, Kansas City, Indianapolis… And wherever Tillie went, Philip Shoberg went too: he was her coach, her manager, her masseur, her press agent and her moral support. In December that year they got married.

> Travelling with her bike and a trunk, she got on trains that crossed the length and breadth of the USA.

And the money started rolling in. When she was working as a seamstress, Tillie earned 3 dollars a week. Winning a race could earn her anything between $200 and $500. There were plenty of generous prizes for the runners up, too. As her fame grew, some organisers paid her $50 just to participate in a race. She was sponsored by the Excelsior Supply Company, a Chicago bike manufacturer which gave her a weekly salary of $25, in addition to a bonus of $200 for every race won. While her mother might have been pleased with the sudden flow of cash coming in, she disapproved of the racing. It wasn't so much the skimpy attire – which provoked some of Tillie's friends to cut off relations with her, 'they really thought I was wicked,' she later said – or the whiff of circus spectacle that coloured these races, but the gambling that went with it that bothered her the most.

Right from the start, Tillie had no illusions about what went on behind the scenes. Just before her first race a man who had been watching the women training sidled up to Tillie and offered her $300 to throw the race and let another rider win – $100 more than what the winner would get. When she told him she had every intention of winning he increased his offer to $500, then $1,000. She learnt someone else had placed a $1,500 bet on her winning, which the man trying to bribe her stood to lose. Tillie, quite disgusted and insulted, determined that he would lose his money (which he did).

There was plenty of rivalry between the women, which the papers made much of. After one race, the *Minneapolis Times* reported Dottie Farnsworth accusing

Tillie of being 'unable to stand the strain. She was given injections of cocaine time and again to ease the pain she experienced and she was almost unable to keep her seat on the wheel the last two days.' By the end of the race, 'Miss Anderson was in a fainting condition when lifted from her wheel, while Miss Farnsworth was in as good shape as the day she started.'

The paper published a response from 'one who was present' who told a very different story: 'After having without any special exertion finished the race an easy winner, Miss Anderson circled the track at least three times and left it without assistance, as can be proved by eye witnesses to the affair. The story regarding the use of injections of cocaine to revive her from exhaustion after the race are absolutely false; on the contrary, Miss Anderson, instead of retiring immediately after the race, as did the rest of the riders, attended an evening party with every appearance of enjoyment.'

One newspaper wrote that: 'Anderson is no such sprinter as Farnsworth or Baldwin, but she is immensely superior to either in strength and she wins her races by tiring out her weaker opponents. She is stronger by far than the average athletic man.'

Other than her husband, Tillie looked somewhat askance at the supposedly 'stronger' sex. Her great niece, Alice Roepke, told me a few stories about Tillie that have become part of the family mythology – she rode in one race featuring male pace-makers and ended up overtaking hers in fury because he was too slow. On another occasion she checked into a hotel with her bike and her trunk. The bellhop didn't fancy his chances lugging the trunk on his own to her room, so nipped across the street to get help. By the time he got back, Tillie in her exasperation had already taken the trunk up herself.

By 1898 Tillie had become unbeatable. Throughout the year, no one could wrest a victory from her, and she won all 19 of the Six-day races she entered. She was inundated with fan mail. Philip subscribed to a cuttings service and as they travelled from city to city, he would cut out and paste all the articles about her – and her rivals – in scrapbooks. By the end of her career there were four of them, consisting of 400 pages, containing thousands of newspaper articles.

And then, over the summer, came the news that Lisette, the great French rider who had recently been crowned world champion, was on her way to America to topple Tillie's crown.

Who was Lisette? According to some sources, she came from Brittany and her name was Amélie le Gall. Other accounts say her name was Lisette Marton (or Martin) and that she came from the Parisian suburb of Puteaux. She was sponsored by the Simpson Lever Chain company and a protégée of the sulphurous Choppy Warburton, notorious even today for doping his riders with strychnine and cocaine. He looks cartoonishly sinister in photos, with his floor-length overcoat, bowler hat and lugubrious gaze. His most famous charges, Arthur Linton and Jimmy Michael, died tragically young, allegedly as a result of the contents of the little black bottles he handed them in races.

Lisette had set speed records for 100km on the road in France in 1894 and 1895, and in 1896 was crowned world champion following an international race at the Royal Aquarium velodrome in Britain. *The Chicago Chronicle* was sniffy about Lisette's exploits, however: 'Her performance of a fraction over nine miles an hour is not remarkable, and in a match race would be considered very slow.'

In one American profile we learn she admired Napoleon Bonaparte and that, 'like all women of genius she had a stubborn little temper that now and then interfered rather seriously with her riding.' Despite the language barrier, Choppy apparently 'understood the little woman's eccentricities better than anybody else in the world.' When she threatened to abandon a race he would do an impression of Napoleon, which supposedly did the trick. In photographs taken by Jules Beau, one of the leading French sports photographers of the day, she is a confident looking woman with precise, neat features who, unlike most of her contemporaries, manages to pull off the mutton sleeve and bloomer look in a way that looks trim, or, as fashion writers might put it, 'together.' In hand written notes compiled later in life, however, Tillie considered Lisette, 'anything but a Paris fashionplate.'

Tillie had been a seamstress and made the most of her cycling outfits. © Alice Olson Foepke Collection

By late August the *Minneapolis Tribune* reported that, 'The wonder of all Europe and the pride of all bicycle enthusiasts walked into Wirtensohn Brothers bicycle store yesterday in company with a portly old gentleman named Monsieur Cascarette. News travels fast, and during their 15-minute visit at the store half the bicyclists of Minneapolis, apparently, came from every direction, and an impromptu reception was held.' Lisette was particularly interested in a photo on the shop's wall of the American champions, and wanted to know which one was Tillie Anderson and which one Lizzie Glaw, before quizzing the

owner about their records. 'When informed that Miss Anderson's record was something over 24 miles in an hour, she gave a tantalizing little laugh, as much as to infer that that was a snail's pace.' The much-hyped Lisette had a talent for playing to the crowds, who were quite taken with the stylish Parisienne, but she was no match for her rivals. There were allegations that in one race three American girls blocked her from getting past, and that Tillie had paid off a weaker American rider, who had no hope of winning, to help set the pace.

On another occasion, Lisette told one newspaper that she had won a race against Tillie, and Tillie responded by putting down a wager, challenging her to ride for either 5 or 25 miles, for either $25 or $250, 'preferably the latter sum', to see who was the strongest. 'Yesterday Miss Anderson said that all of the races at these cities were Six-day races and that the French champion female cyclist defeated her in one heat only,' the paper reported. 'Miss Anderson won the first prize, and, therefore, is the champion. If she is not the champion she wants to know and this race is to decide.' Lisette, it was pointed out, 'has never succeeded in winning a Six-day race since coming to the United States and, if Anderson can help it, never will.'

Tillie's career may have been flying, but home life was another matter. In 1899 her husband was diagnosed with tuberculosis and went to Europe for several months in an attempt to improve his health. The stress of travelling and racing, of negotiating contracts and managing the press would have been too much for most riders to handle on their own, let alone in a state of anxiety regarding their husband's health. She engaged a manager and soldiered on, with an ambitious programme of 28 races that year, of which 12 were Six-day events. Despite her anxieties regarding Philip and their future, she lost only three races.

On his way back to America Philip's ship hit an iceberg. Tillie was in the middle of a Six-day race in Zanesville, Ohio. Somehow the boat managed to stay afloat and limp into New York. With the new century, Philip moved to California in the hope the climate would help. Tillie continued to zig-zag the country on her own, winning 13 out of 14 races. The following year she took part in 19 races, winning 18.

In 1902, she did eight races and won them all, but it was a year marked by tragedy. Her arch-rival, Dottie Farnsworth, died as a result of an accident on the track. It was a wonder there hadn't been a fatality sooner, and it brought home to the general public quite how dangerous the sport could be. It's often reported that Dottie's death led to women's racing being banned, but Roger Gilles has been unable to find the evidence for these claims.

Whether or not Farnsworth's death was the catalyst, women's racing ground to an abrupt halt. Fans had already been losing interest and the mania had passed. Once the epitome of speed, bikes were now being overtaken by motorbikes and cars. More poignantly for Tillie, 1902 was marked by Philip's death. Suddenly she was bereft of both the man who meant everything to her and the career which defined her. It must have been a devastating blow.

Tillie, however, kept going, drawing on deep reserves of Swedish Lutheran stoicism. She earned a living giving Swedish massage, something she had learnt from Philip. In 1909 she bought herself a car and enjoyed travelling great distances with it. She built herself a little wood cabin on a fishing resort in Minnesota that her sister and husband had set up, and looked after their children as if they were her own.

She never remarried. She continued riding her bike, and in the 1930s was a key figure in the development of Chicago's bicycle networks. She lived to a fine old age, dying aged 90 on 29 April 1965. Over the years, her great niece Alice has campaigned to have her achievements recognised. It is thanks to Alice that Tillie was inducted to the US Bicycling Hall of Fame as its first female rider of the 19th century. She was the catalyst behind Gilles' book, and has generously given journalists and writers access to the wealth of material she left behind. Tillie's archive confounds all our modern assumptions regarding women and sport of the time. Even though she lived in different cities and spent many years travelling, she kept all her mementoes, as if she was a preserving a voice that could speak to us directly from the past.

> Tillie, however, kept going, drawing on deep reserves of Swedish Lutheran stoicism.

HÉLÈNE DUTRIEUX

'The Human Arrow'

Hélène Dutrieux was a pint-sized thrill-seeker who very early in life decided she wasn't going to bother with accepted ideas of how a woman should behave. She lived in an age when 'polite' women's fashions prevented them from moving or even breathing freely, when it was considered unbecoming for a woman to work, or to break into a sweat, or to express an opinion on anything that wasn't essentially domestic. Dutrieux became, in turn: a world champion cyclist, a stuntwoman, an actress, a record-breaking pilot, an ambulance driver, a hospital director and, finally, a journalist.

In a publicity shot of Hélène (pictured left), taken in the 1890s for Dunlop tyres, she's track-standing on a bike with a monster chain that looks like it could saw your leg off. Looking directly into the camera, here's a woman not just in control of her bike, but also her destiny. Hélène did everything on her own terms. She refused to fly at one aviation meet until the organisers increased her fees. She didn't hesitate to sue a manufacturer who failed to supply her with a plane. She caused a scandal by casually letting drop that she didn't wear corsets. She had no qualms making deals with competing theatres when her own wasn't giving her enough work. And it wasn't until 1922 – when she was 45 – that she finally decided to get married. 'The man who wants me must catch me in the air,' she'd teased her legions of fans.

She was 'a most charming young lady,' wrote one reporter, 'with a graceful step, who on first impressions would appear to be one of those fragile creatures with a talent for flirting and a carefree life. But behind that pleasantly feminine appearance, Miss Dutrieu [sic] hides an absolutely masculine energy.'

Hélène Dutrieux (or Dutrieu, as she would later become known in France) was born in Tournai in the French-speaking part of Belgium, a few kilometres from the French border, on 10 July 1877. Her family later moved to Lille, where she left school to start working at the age of 14. Her father was an army officer and she had an older brother, Eugène, who became a professional cyclist and circus director. It's not clear when or how Hélène started riding, but by 1895, when she was only 18, she set a new world hour record. In 1896 she became World Champion at a track meet in Ostende, covering 2km in 4 minutes and 31 seconds. That same year she won a 12-day race in London, in the second year of its existence, held at the Royal Aquarium, an imposing building opened in 1876 and featuring a soaring glass and steel roof, a stone's throw from Westminster

Abbey. The cycle races were held on a banked wooden indoor track on which riders covered ten laps for every mile.

In the course of the 12 days, riders took part in a variety of events, including a Six-day race, before an overall winner emerged. Sometimes as many as 30 riders would compete – champions from England, Scotland, France, Belgium, the Netherlands and even Canada – and since they couldn't all be safely accommodated on such a small track at the same time, they would be split into groups riding at different times of day. The racing was nonetheless dangerous, with crashes a constant feature, and the numbers would be whittled down when injuries forced riders to abandon. Each day, the best riders would accumulate well over 50 miles in the course of three and a half hours' racing.

For Dutrieux to win the 12-day race in London, she would have needed many qualities, including endurance, the ability to 'spurt,' or put on a sustained attack over several laps, technical mastery of the bike and the awkwardly designed track in London (which had been criticised by many cycling publications), an ability to anticipate and avoid accidents, tactical nous and a readiness to form alliances in order to block rivals, and perhaps most importantly, robust nerves.

In 1897 Dutrieux won the world championship, and when she was 21 she had won the Grand Prix d'Europe and was awarded the Cross of St André with diamonds, by King Leopold II of Belgium, in recognition of her achievements.

Dutrieux was one of many exceptional women racing in Europe and America in the 1890s who were able to earn a good living through prize money and sponsorship deals. Dutrieux herself was sponsored by the Simpson Chain company, as were her rivals, 'Lisette' and 'Miss Grace.' Their names received top billing in Simpson adverts, ahead of male stars like Constant Huret and Arthur Linton, both winners of Bordeaux–Paris.

Unlike their male counterparts, who had city-to-city road-races in which to compete, like Paris–Roubaix or Liège–Bastogne–Liège, women's racing at this point seems to have been confined to velodromes. This had the effect of making it an accessible spectator sport, although not all the spectators were interested in the racing alone. Many commentators were shocked at the indecency of scantily dressed women whirling around the track and breaking into a sweat in such close proximity to predominantly male spectators. The events also attracted gamblers, and were considered to have no more status than circus spectacles.

That's not to say the women didn't take the racing seriously, though. Most of them had male coaches or managers who had often been champions themselves. The women paid attention to their diet, did strength training, and as the decade progressed, jettisoned their stiff jackets with mutton leg sleeves, corsets and pantaloons in favour of more aerodynamic, close-fitting sweaters, knitted shorts and tights.

And then, just as in America, the scene died out with the start of the new century. Race organisers had become complacent and ineffective, and audiences found new distractions, like motion pictures, motorbikes and cars. By 1903, the Royal Aquarium had lost so much money its owners had gone bankrupt and the building was sold and demolished.

In July 1903, while the inaugural Tour de France was underway, Dutrieux was stunt riding, cycling a loop of a vertical track in Marseille. That was nothing compared to her next trick, performed two months later. Calling herself 'La Flèche Humaine' – the human arrow – she devised an indoor stunt in which, from a height of 18 metres, she'd hurtle down a steep, narrow ramp with no protective railing, then launch into the air, before landing 15 metres later where the ramp resumed. With this sensational stunt she went on tour, performing in cities like Paris, London and Berlin. 'It is the most breathless business,' reported a British publication, *The Star*, in 1904. 'The swiftness and the daring of it leave the audience almost stunned.' The applause, once spectators had recovered their senses, 'shakes the big glass roof so far overhead.'

> Speed and daring were to become her defining qualities, only the means with which she expressed them evolved.

Attuned to her time, Dutrieux was already onto the next thing. Speed and daring were to become her defining qualities, only the means with which she expressed them evolved. Within the same year Dutrieux had introduced a motorbike into the stunt, which was now renamed 'La Motocyclette Ailée' – the winged motorbike – with which she was performing in Berlin when an accident forced her to spend several months recovering.

During this period she became an actress, taking on primarily comic roles in Parisian theatres such as the Théâtre de Capucines and the Théâtre des Mathurins. Around the same time, she was also racing cars for the manufacturer Clement-Bayard. It's not clear how successful her acting or car racing was, but it was enough to maintain a public profile, ensuring that her name was mentioned in society gossip columns when they listed the notable personalities who attended parties.

In 1908, Clément-Bayard invited her to become a test pilot for their first airplane. Aviation was in its infancy; in January that year Henri Farman became the first Frenchman to fly a kilometre. Clément-Bayard were promoting a lightweight monoplane, called the *Démoiselle,* developed by a Brazilian engineer called Santos-Dumont. It would be the world's first series produced plane, a tiny 'entry

level' model that could in theory sell in large quantities. Clément-Bayard needed a lightweight pilot. Weighing only 45 kilos, Dutrieux fitted the bill.

It would be a win-win situation for both parties: for Dutrieux, who had turned 31, it was a means to prolong her career and increase her fame. For Clément-Bayard, there was not just the publicity value of a charming actress, celebrated stunt woman and champion cyclist promoting their plane, but the subliminal message for their primarily male customers: if a mere slip of a *woman* can fly this, so can you.

The transition from cyclist to aviator was in fact a common one; many aviation pioneers had been racing cyclists, including Lucien Lesna, who'd won Paris-Roubaix in 1901 and 1902, and two of the three Farman brothers, Henry and Maurice, who became pioneering manufacturers and engineers. Dutrieux wasn't the only woman recruited to fly the *Démoiselle*, either; another successful bike racer from the 1890s, who went by the stage name of 'Miss Aboukaia,' was a second test pilot.

Once again, Dutrieux threw herself into a hazardous occupation; in the early years of aviation, horrible deaths were commonplace. No matter how skilled the pilot, every flight was a game of Russian roulette; engines commonly failed, causing a plane to plummet from the sky, or the wind could suddenly turn, causing the machine flip over when it landed. Pilots died falling out at altitude, got crushed or were consumed in a ball of fire.

Dutrieux's first flight was to take place in December 1908. Her training consisted of a few words of advice from a mechanic shortly before climbing into the plane, and then she was off, shooting up into the air, only to crash shortly thereafter, having suddenly panicked and descended too fast. The plane was destroyed, but not Hélène's confidence.

By April 1909 she was able to fly on her own. A few months later the Aéro Club de France decided to make it obligatory for pilots to have a licence, and as a result, flying schools opened up across the country. Dutrieux took lessons with the Farman brothers and in 1910 became the fourth woman in the world, and the first Belgian, to hold a licence. In the meantime, Dutrieux set a women's distance record flight of 45km completed in 40 minutes between Holland and Belgium.

Bored now of the *Demoiselle* and its limited possibilities, she approached another manufacturer, Roger Sommer, asking to fly a new biplane he had built, which was a much more powerful machine. After a successful test flight in April 1910, Dutrieux had the plane transported to an aviation exhibition in Odessa, where, flying low, she hit a chimney and crashed again. Dutrieux was catapulted out of her seat but was lucky to survive with just a few bruises. The plane, however, was a write-off.

When Dutrieux returned to Paris, ready to participate in other lucrative European events, Sommer broke his contract and refused to supply her with a new set of wings, justifying the decision with the fact she didn't have a licence. Dutrieux sued him for 100,000 francs (approximately €388,000 in today's money), but eventually only won 5,000. A report on the trial some two years later in *Le Journal* quotes Sommer's lawyer stating, 'Before the plane was repaired, Mr Sommer agreed to resume teaching Miss Dutrieu. But given the results were completely negative, it seemed dangerous to him to let her fly off on solo adventures. Hence his refusal to supply her with a machine.'

'And yet,' countered Dutrieux's lawyer, 'Mr Sommer should remember that Miss Dutrieu, has, since her débuts in aviation, demonstrated herself to be particularly talented in this sport, that she achieved her licence with brilliance, and that she has accomplished, especially in Belgium, the most remarkable performances.'

> Over the next few years, Dutrieux ruled the skies.

Over the next few years, Dutrieux ruled the skies. At the end of 1910 she won the inaugural *Coupe Fémina*, created by a women's magazine of the same name, for the longest flight achieved by a woman, which she obtained by covering 60.8km in just over an hour. The Farman brothers became her sponsors, and her benefits would include a chauffeur driven car and two mechanics and, it seems, all the spare planes and motors she needed.

Her achievements include winning the *Coppa del Rei* trophy in Italy in the endurance category, beating not only the women but also the men. She continually broke women's records for altitude and distance. After losing the *Coupe Fémina* to her rival, another remarkable sports woman, Marie Marvingt, she reclaimed it again in 1911, this time covering a distance of 254.8km, in just under three hours. In 1912 she became the first woman to pilot a seaplane, a much more technically challenging machine, drawing crowds to her exhibition flights over the lake at Enghien-les-Bains, a spa town North of Paris.

In 1913 she was the first female pilot awarded the French *Légion d'Honneur*, an extremely rare honour for a woman (and a foreigner, to boot). Then, just as with her cycling career, her piloting years came to an abrupt end, this time with the start of the First World War. Dutrieux became an ambulance driver for the French Red Cross. The army sent her to America to give propaganda talks, and on her return, she directed the Val de Grâce military hospital until the end of the war.

Left: Charming, cheerful and fearless. And the first Belgian female pilot. © Library of Congress Washington DC

After the war she became a journalist, and in 1922 took on French citizenship when she married Pierre Mortier, a novelist, playwright and editor of *Gil Blas,* a celebrated literary magazine. The newspaper's archives suggest they must have already been acquainted for at least ten years, although during that period Mortier was living with another woman, an actress with whom he had a daughter in 1915. The Mortiers bought a chateau in Colombes, in the Brie region South East of Paris, and a few years later he became the local mayor and a member of the Radical Socialist party.

An influential figure in regional politics, he held his post until the Second World War and German occupation, when he was removed from office for being Jewish. Mortier escaped to the US, where he joined the resistance under de Gaulle's leadership. Dutrieux, meanwhile, went to London. They both survived the war, but Mortier died of cancer shortly afterwards in 1946. Hélène went back to Paris, where she re-engaged with the aviation world. She became vice president of the women's section of the *Aéro-Club de France* and established an eponymous prize for female pilots from France and Belgium.

Hélène Dutrieux died on 12 June 1961, a month short of her 84th birthday, exactly two months after Yuri Gagarin had become the first person to venture into space. Throughout her life, Dutrieux saw where the future lay. Even if flying became her true passion, cycling had opened the door for her. It had represented the apotheosis of a moment of technical innovation at the end of the 19th century, and her embrace of it lead her onto ever more sophisticated speed machines that would end up defining modern life.

LA "MOTO AILÉE"

Mlle Dutrieu dans la " Moto ailée ".

Voici en quoi consiste cet audacieux numéro, importé à Paris par Mlle Hélène Dutrieu, la charmante artiste, célèbre autrefois sur les vélodromes, et qui abandonna la piste pour la scène et les acrobaties sportives. Montée sur une légère motocyclette, elle descend du cintre en suivant une étroite piste qui, arrivée près du sol, se recourbe et s'arrête brusquement. Elle est alors projetée presque verticalement dans le vide et vient retomber sur une plate-forme située à 15 mètres plus haut. Ce numéro, que l'on a pu voir pendant quelques jours dans un music-hall parisien, a été interrompu par ordre de la préfecture de police, comme trop dangereux. Un soir, en effet, l'audacieuse cycliste dévia de la ligne droite, manqua la plate-forme et ne dut son salut qu'à sa présence d'esprit, qui lui permit de saisir de la main gauche une corde, pendant que sa machine allait s'abîmer dans les fauteuils d'orchestre.

ALFONSINA STRADA

'The Devil in a Skirt'

It was when 14-year-old Alfonsina Morini came home with a live piglet that she had won in a bike race, that her mother finally decided she'd had enough. Why did her daughter insist on bringing the whole family into disrepute with this shameful, unladylike sport? Only heaven knew how much Signora Morini laboured to keep her growing family – not to mention the orphans she took in from time to time for some spare cash – not only fed and clothed, but also polite, literate and law-abiding. And what gratitude did she ever get from this headstrong girl, with her unreasonable obsession with this infernal machine? Her second child, what's more, who should be giving a good example to her younger siblings. Oh, the shame of it!

The century was only five years old, and bicycles were still something exotic in the countryside of Emilia Romagna outside Bologna.

But there's no point in shutting the shed door after the cyclist has departed. Since the age of 10, when her father had brought home a bike he'd swapped for some chickens with the local doctor, Alfonsina had been discovering the thrill of cycling: the speed, the wind in her hair, the sense of herself it gave her, in contrast to the anonymity of life in a vast tribe. Alfonsina was not letting anyone take away the great pleasure she felt as she accelerated on the long flat road out of Fossamarza and kept riding for miles and miles. She thrilled to the strength in her muscles, just as much as she took pride in the quiet respect of the young lads she encountered in the country races, astounded at the abilities of this compact, chunky ball of muscle and determination.

'There goes *the Devil in a skirt*,' the local villagers would mutter. For what else could you call a girl on the threshold of womanhood who preferred to go riding dressed in a man's skimpy shorts and figure-hugging jersey, over spending all day in the kitchen making tortellini or attending Mass? Even worse, who *lied* to her mother that she was attending Mass, when she was sneaking off to races? Nothing good would ever come of it.

It wasn't long before Alfonsina was shunted off to nearby Bologna, where she started an apprenticeship as a seamstress. But she carried on riding her bike – presumably also cycling the 13 or so kilometres to work every day. Sometimes she would come across professional riders out training and would ride with them. They were astonished by her nerve and even more astounded when they tried but failed to drop her. Invariably these meetings led to questions. 'How did she learn to ride a bike?' they would ask, and 'How did she get so strong?' 'What's it's like, being a proper racing cyclist?' Alfonsina would ask in return, and more importantly 'Where do you race?'

The Tour de France was two years old. Cycling in Italy was in its infancy. The great Giro di Lombardia, initially called Milano-Milano, would be launched in November. Between 1905 and 1910 a host of famous races would emerge: Milan–Mantua (1906), Milan–Sanremo (1907), Milan–Modena (1908), the Giro d'Italia (1909), the Circuito Emiliano and the Giri del Piemonte, del Veneto, di Romagna, dell'Umbria, della Campania...

The country folk of Emilia might laugh at a girl speeding about on a bike, but there were other cities where women took cycling seriously, and even raced, such as Turin, where great crowds turned out on Sundays to watch them battle it out on the Piazza d'Armi and in the Parco del Valentina.

So Alfonsina took her bike and got on the train to Turin, more than 300km away, and started racing, and winning. The great champion of the day was called Giuseppina Carignano and in 1907, at the age of only 16, Alfonsina beat her, too. She became celebrated as the 'Best Woman Cyclist in Italy.'

When she was racing on the track, the women's events usually took place after the men's, which is how Alfonsina met Carlo Messori, a big strapping lad ten years her senior, also from Emilia Romagna. In 1908 he would break a world record in the 500m standing start and he was one of three riders nicknamed the '*tre M della velocità*', or the three speedy Ms.

> She wanted to make a career of it, to bask in the fame of being both a champion and pioneer, to show just what a woman could do.

Messori took Alfonsina under his wing, giving her valuable training and racing advice. In 1909 he was invited to the Grand Prix St Petersburg and persuaded Alfonsina to come too. She was such a sensation that Tsar Nicholas II presented her with a special medal in recognition of her talent. Back in Italy, cycling was in the process of forging its identity, and Alfonsina had every intention of being part of it. It was her obsession. She wanted to make a career of it, to bask in the fame of being both a champion and pioneer, to show just what a woman could do. From her own race results she knew the relentless rhetoric about women's inherent fragility was, frankly, just a load of baloney – she might not be men's equal, but she could hold her own in their company. So Alfonsina also raced in country events that were open to anyone. In one of these she made headlines for being the only woman racing amongst 50 men, and coming 7th.

She really put herself on the map in 1911 when she set a new women's hour record in Moncalieri, south of Turin, covering a distance of 37.192km, improving on a previous record of 36.793km set in 1903 by a French rider called Louise Roger. To put that in perspective, when the UCI finally began officially recording women's record attempts in 1955, the first rider to claim the hour was the Russian Tamara Novikova, who managed a distance of 38.473km. We don't know what sort of bike Alfonsina rode for her record attempt in 1911, but we can safely assume it was a good deal heavier and more primitive than Novikova's, some 45 years later.

Alfonsina moved to Milan, the heart of Italian cycling, where she met Luigi Strada who was also in love with the sport. A wood engraver by profession, Luigi was also a tinkerer, a man who liked to invent things, take gadgets apart and improve them. So in addition to his engraving business he had a workshop fixing bikes.

Luigi was absolutely taken with this curly haired marvel of strength and speed. Here in Milan, where the artists of the Futurist movement were ruffling feathers with their aggressive manifestos celebrating speed and technology, embracing the new and pouring scorn on stuffy old notions of taste and manners, here he had found a marvellous girl who epitomised devil-may-care modernity.

They set up house together and Luigi became Alfonsina's champion, riding and training with her, promoting her and accompanying her to races.

In Milan she also met Fabio Orlandini, the Paris correspondent of the *Gazzetta dello Sport,* which led to Alfonsina being invited to take part in a series of races between 1912 and 1914 at the Vélodrome Buffalo, the Vélodrome d'Hiver and the Parc des Princes. The French press dubbed her 'la Lisette Italienne' – *the Italian Lisette*, in reference to their great star from the 1890s, who had since gone to seek her fortune in America.

With the start of the First World War she went back to Italy, now aged 23, with one idea in mind. The money and acclaim from racing against women on the track was good, but it wasn't enough, and it certainly didn't have any great status. She wanted to take part in 'real' races, the ones on the road, against men.

But first, on 24 October 1915, at the age of 24, she married Luigi. He gave her a fancy new racing bike as a wedding present. Alfonsina now became Signora Strada, or Mrs Road, a name so perfect you'd be tempted to assume she'd invented it.

In 1917 she set her sights on the Giro di Lombardia, then in its 12th year. Alfonsina turned up at the offices of the *Gazetta dello Sport*, which organised the race, in order to sign up for the 204km event. The idea was so preposterous that Armando Cougnet, the race director, naturally refused. But Alfonsina had done her homework: there was nothing in the rules about the race being men-only, she pointed out, and anyway, she was a 2nd category amateur, and so was technically eligible. Cougnet presumably scratched his head, shrugged his shoulders and said, '*d'accordo.*'

The war might still have been raging, but many of the top pre-war champions were present on the start line. They included the Belgian Philippe Thys, who had won the Tour de France in 1913 and 1914, the French champion Henri Pélissier, who had come second in the Tour in 1913, and Costante Girardengo, the emerging Italian '*campionissimo*', and Pélissier's great rival.

Thys won the race by a hair's breadth over Pélissier and Alfonsina came 32nd, and last, one and a half hours behind them. She finished in the company of two other riders, Pietro Sigbaldi and Gino Augé. Five other riders finished in the preceding two minutes. Of the 54 riders who set off, 22 had abandoned. It was, in fact, an extremely impressive performance, which won her the respect and friendship of Girardengo.

The following year she was back. This time she had been invited, no doubt for the publicity value her presence would bring to a dramatically depleted race. Taking place just a week after the end of the war, numbers were even lower than the previous year, with only 36 riders turning up at the start. This time the race was 190km long, and was won by Gaetano Belloni, Girardengo's main Italian rival, with an average speed of 26.635km/h.

Alfonsina finished second to last, outsprinting the last rider, Carlo Colombo. The peloton had essentially split into two groups, and she was in second bunch of seven riders who finished only 23 minutes behind the winner, while more than a third of the overall field abandoned.

Eberardo Pavesi, who would later become Gino Bartali's Directeur Sportif, had been riding in the second bunch when he heard a rider coming up behind. 'I turned and saw it was Alfonsina. She was riding at my side and started saying, "Come on, Pavesi, let's go and get those guys up

Fresh-faced and determined looking. © BtA

front." "Are you crazy Alfonsina?" I said. "We've already tried and there's nothing doing."' A little later the bunch came up to a banner signalling a *prime* up ahead, at which point Alfonsina piped up again. 'Come on, Pavesi, when we get to the banner, lead me out for the sprint.' Another ridiculous request, as far as Pavesi was concerned, but, 'I buried myself with a kilometre to go and she held my wheel with incredible ease,' he remembered. 'With 50 metres to go, I took her by the saddle and pushed her forward a few metres ahead of us, and the crowds roared as if she'd won the Tour of Lombardy.'

When sports writers weren't ignoring these early female riders, there was a tendency to write about them in comedic tones, as if they were a slapstick side-show to the main event. Alfonsina was clearly considered an out-of-place eccentric and there were plenty of patronising jokes and lascivious cartoons about her in the press at the time. Since she didn't play by the rules of how women should behave, she wasn't treated with the respect usually accorded to women. Many spectators whistled and jeered and made salacious comments. Others complained that her very presence, denigrated the serious nature of such a hard sport. But there is nothing comic about her achievements.

Legend has it that in 1924 she snuck her way into the Giro d'Italia pretending to be a man. In fact it was the race organisers who invited her. Emilio Colombo and Armando Cougnet, the editor and manager of the *Gazetta dello Sport,* were in a bit of a spot. The teams were essentially on strike, having insisted on a participation fee, which the *Gazetta* had refused. So now the paper faced the prospect of a race with no stars and little interest for readers. A new rival, the *Corriere dello Sport*, was making inroads into its readership – and profits. Thinking of the publicity potential of having a woman in the race, Colombo and Cougnet invited Alfonsina to take part. She didn't need asking twice. They signed her up with the man's name, Alfonsin, and it was only when the race began that it became apparent that there was a woman in the riders' midst.

'Alfonsina doesn't challenge anybody for victory, she just wants to show that even the weaker sex can do the same as strong men,' wrote the *Gazetta* in one of its editorials portraying her as a feminist who, by her example, was leading the charge for women's suffrage, which Mussolini would partly introduce the following year.

This was by far her toughest physical challenge: the race featured 3,613km ridden over 12 stages. These averaged just over 300km. The longest individual stage was 415km long. In order to arrive at the finish in time for journalists' reports to go in the next day's editions, the stages invariably began at night. The roads were mostly unsurfaced, and frequently went over mountains. Every day she lost time: on stage one (300km) she finished fourth to last, two and half hours behind the winner. On stage two (307.9km) she finished near the back again, this time 2h6m5s behind the winner. On the third stage (284km) she was fourth from last again, 2h33m38s behind the winner. And so it continued. At the same time, riders abandoned every day. By the end of stage three, 30 of them had left the race.

The editors had done well in calculating Alfonsina's appeal to readers. 'In only two stages, this little lady's popularity has become greater than all the missing champions put together', the paper reported. In Rome at the end of stage three she was invited to a number of receptions held in her honour and was given presents, including a fancy new jersey and some earrings. 'She is radiant', declared the *Gazetta*. The *tifosi* couldn't get enough of her and, she was buoyed by their presence as the race grew increasingly difficult. They would wait – sometimes for hours – by the roadside for her to come through, long after the champions had passed. After one stage they hoisted her off her bike at the finish and carried her on their shoulders.

> 'In only two stages, this little lady's popularity has become greater than all the missing champions put together.'

Disaster struck on the 8th stage, the second day in the Apennines. The weather was hellish, as were the roads, as riders struggled along in the wind, rain and mud. Alfonsina crashed with such force that her handlebars broke. Cobbling something together with a broom pole, she managed to complete the stage. Yet no matter how valiant her efforts, she was almost four hours behind the stage winner, and struck off the race.

Perhaps the naysayers had been right; maybe the Giro really was too much for a woman. There were other disadvantages because of her sex: the masseurs considered her a low priority among the riders, so she only got a quick, perfunctory rub down when everyone else had been looked after. She couldn't get access to the shared washrooms until everyone had gone to bed. She made no friends and got no help from other riders, since no one wanted the shame of finishing behind her. Even the greatest champions have their limits, and Alfonsina it seemed had finally reached hers. Now she was out, she might as well pack up and go home.

For Colombo this was a disaster: thanks to Alfonsina the paper was selling like hot cakes, but he couldn't have one set of rules for her and another for the lads. If she was out, she was out. But he was also a businessman, and where money is at stake, a compromise is always possible. So Colombo proposed to Alfonsina that she continue riding, just to complete the race, even if she might no be longer eligible for the GC. In return she would receive 500 lire for her efforts, donated by the newspaper's readers. How could she refuse? So she forged on, further mishaps notwithstanding, all the way to the 12th and final stage. Ninety riders had set out from Milan. Only 30 returned, and she was one of them.

Alfonsina continued to race, even though she was not invited back to the Giro. By 1925 Colombo and Cougnet had settled things with the teams and they had their stars back. Alfonsina had served her purpose admirably the previous year, but she was surplus to requirements now. She never really retired from the sport. In the 1930s she was taking part in 'unofficial' world championship races in Belgium organized by a maverick race promoter, Jos De Stobbeleire. It's said that she won 36 races against men in the course of her career.

Her life was not easy, however. Luigi suffered from a 'mental collapse' and spent the rest of his days in a mental institution, which ate up most of the money she made following her Giro ride. He died in 1946. Four years later Alfonsina remarried, this time to Carlo Messori, the track rider who'd taken her to St Petersburg so many years before. Carlo, too, had been recently widowed. Had they always had a special spark? Was this happiness at last? They ran a bike shop together, and went to watch the races. Carlo clearly adored his wife, and wrote her biography. Much to his chagrin no publisher would accept the manuscript. They didn't have long together: Messori died in 1957.

Alfonsina was left on her own, with her two-room apartment above the shop, and her Moto Guzzi motorbike.

After going to watch a race, the Tre Valle Varesine, she suddenly collapsed one day outside her apartment, with her motorbike falling on top of her. She had suffered a fatal heart attack at the age of 68. Alfonsina Strada was – and remains – the only woman ever to have taken part in a men's Grand Tour race. This alone is utterly remarkable. But even more, we should celebrate the circumstances in which she did this. She was born in the 19th century, into a traditional rural community with old-world mores. The Italy she grew up in was dominated by the powerful forces of Catholicism, Socialism and Fascism, none of which had any interest in boosting women's causes. It is hard to conceive now of what it must have been like living as an independent, free-spirited woman in such a suffocating culture. Alfonsina stuck her head above the parapet when competitive women's cycling barely existed and constantly pushed for greater challenges. She rode 300km-long stages at a time when the UCI didn't even think women should be racing 3km. Her achievements in this context are nothing less than staggering.

'Miss Modern'

Evelyn Hamilton was a rider with several names, and, it seems, quite a few life stories, not all of them entirely plausible. Did she work for the French Resistance? Was her bike shop the headquarters for a network of spies? Was she related to the Pélissier brothers, of whom the oldest, Henri, won the *Tour de France*? Or was she, quite simply, a talented and very photogenic rider with a penchant for spinning yarns?

Whatever Hamilton did or said, she was the first British celluloid celebrity cyclist. During the 1930s Pathé couldn't get enough of her on their newsreels. There are films featuring her on Herne Hill velodrome; racing, being paced behind a derny, warming up on a home trainer or demonstrating the benefits of skipping. She had legs that go on forever, a wardrobe of natty ribbed sweaters, a stylish blonde bob and a penchant for berets worn at a jaunty angle. She was simply and straightforwardly cool – not just a pretty thing (even when she's filmed rather gratuitously in a bikini) but a real rider, evident from her smooth pedalling style on the track or her dexterous stunts on the road in one film on safe cycling. A favourite bit of footage sees her setting out to ride the 700 miles from London to John o' Groats. The camera looks down from a height as she heads out of town, accompanied by a great peloton of adoring 'boyke friends', as the narrator calls them.

In many of these films she was called Miss Gladys Hamilton, which is confusing because her first name was Evelyn and she was technically a 'Mrs'. She was born Eveline Alice Alexandra Bayliss in Westminster on 3 April 1906, but later changed her first name to Evelyn. She had four older brothers. Her father was a policeman and her mother died when she was only 15. At the age of 20 she married a fruiterer's assistant called John Henry Hamilton. Jack – as he was known – was a keen cyclist (whether they met through the sport, or one got the other into it, is not clear) and he and Evelyn went tandem touring in their early years together. They had a child in 1927 who died when he was only 10 months old.

She was indeed a champion. In 1931 she won the first women's half-mile sprint handicap and the Sporting Life trophy at the old Stamford Bridge cinder track. In September 1934 she set off to ride 1000 miles in seven days, riding a Claud Butler – he later marketed a women's-specific light weight racing frame inspired by her, which he named 'Miss Modern'. A year later she rode 700 miles from

London to John o' Groats in four and a half days. In August 1938 the press report on her completing the challenge of riding 10,000 miles in a 100 days.

Then there are other records that are harder to verify. In one Pathé film we are told she had won 50 races in France, England and Belgium. In a cutting from a Birmingham paper from 1934 we read she also won a London to Brighton walking race.

We do know she was a rare professional female rider, which means that she accepted sponsorship, but doesn't necessarily mean that she could have lived off that income. More significantly, as a 'professional' she would have been excluded from racing in the UK, which was a strictly amateur-only scene. Hamilton travelled abroad to get her racing fix. She wouldn't have been the only British rider to do so: around the same time another long-distance specialist, Lilian Dredge, was also travelling to international road races in Belgium.

If Evelyn was so talented, why did she forgo her amateur status? I suspect she understood she was good but not one of the best – and realised there was money to be made and alternative glory to be had in doing highly publicised rides and appearing on the screen; relatively early in her career she was a body double for Gracie Fields in the film *Sing As We Go*. British bike manufacturing was also experiencing a boom, and Claud Butler was not the only manufacturer who paid Hamilton to promote his bikes. She was frequently called on to promote home trainers to housewives as a way to 'keep fit and stay trim' (in between presumably starching sheets and feeding the baby).

In any case, she clearly had a talent for working the publicity machine. In 1938 she went into business herself, and together with Jack set up a bike shop under her name, at 416A Streatham High Road. It continued well into the late 1960s.

So far, we can be fairly confident about the plausibility of her story, give or take perhaps some details on her race palmarès. With the outbreak of the war, however, things took a strange turn. According to interviews she did later in life, and internet hearsay, Hamilton was stuck in Paris – there are stories that she was doing a 'wall of death' stunt in a circus – when the Germans arrived. She is said to have ended up in the French Resistance, secretly ferrying people across Paris on a tandem. She is supposed to have lived with a Frenchman called Fernand Maurice Helsen, ending up on a wanted list and taking a dead woman's identity to avoid being caught. She worked in a café frequented by the Gestapo. Her shop in London became a headquarters for a militant spy network that was part of the French Resistance, and was run by three French men, one of whom, it's claimed, was one of the Pélissier brothers. She was captured by the Germans, but having taken the wise precaution of hiding a miniature pistol in her hair which was tied into a bun, she was able to shoot her captor and flee back to Britain.

She was – it seems – awarded the Cross of Lorraine by General de Gaulle after the war, which was an honour given to members of the Resistance. The word 'Lorraine Cycles' and the motif of a Lorraine cross, adopted by the Resistance as a counter symbol to the Swastika, featured on the badges of the bikes which she sold under her name. But then, it seems the Cross of Lorraine was only awarded to French citizens and I have been unable to find her name on a list of those who received it.

Even if she hadn't actually received this honour, it's not impossible she was involved in the Resistance. It wasn't until some years after the death of the great Italian champion, Gino Bartali, in 2000, that it emerged he had carried out many heroic acts to save Jewish lives, including couriering secret documents in his bike frame. Matt Rendell's biography of José Beyaert, the colourful and somewhat dodgy French rider who became Olympic champion in 1948, describes how guerrilla elements of the Resistance would force professional riders to work for them as couriers, sometimes even carrying weapons in their musettes. And finally, if all that spy fiction is to be believed, beautiful women make excellent spies. Evelyn would have been perfect in that respect – she clearly liked men, moved in a male-dominated world, and if the gossip about her is true, had many lovers.

Back in London, after the war, we are on more secure ground. She sponsored a men's team in 1947 which took part in a Brighton to Glasgow stage race which would have been organised by the British League of Racing Cyclists, the controversial breakaway cycling body which introduced massed start road racing to Britain during the war. It seems appropriate that Evelyn would have sided with the rebels. There's a rather 'racy' picture in the Sunday Post of one of her riders who had come second, Johnny Raine, embracing 'The Boss' with his arm wrapped around her, pulling her close, while planting a big smacker on the lips – it's certainly not a polite peck on the cheek.

In 1952 she was back on her bike, this time breaking her 10,000 miles in 100 days record by covering 12,000 miles, with the aim 'To show that British cycle equipment is still the world's best and that women can keep pace with men.'

She died aged 99 in 2005, and is buried in Swaffham in Norfolk. On her gravestone the name reads Evelyn Alice Helsen, and the Lorraine Cross makes another appearance.

There are many accounts of her story online, mostly without references, adding to the difficulty of sifting fact from fiction. One of the most convincing accounts I have found is written by Michael Townsend, whom we have to thank for a lot of research into her history. He is a member of the Veteran Cycle Club, and his collection of some 27 bikes from the 1930s to the 1950s contains an Evelyn Hamilton model.

Townsend is somewhat sceptical about her wartime stories, many of which she recounted in local press interviews in her retirement. They don't all add up, but there are enough elements of reality in them to make them beguiling. Helsen for example, did exist. He was of French origin and born in Paris, but his parents moved to London at the turn of the century. It's unlikely that he was in Paris during the war, but he did work in the French Embassy. It's quite possible that he and Evelyn were lovers, but less likely that they married, since he was a Catholic with a wife and two children.

Evelyn and Jack are thought to have separated at some point during the war, although later in life they were on friendly terms and he would visit her in Swaffham, where it's said she continued to have affairs, including one with the landlord of her local pub.

Claud Butler is said to have been another of her many *amoureux*, and it would seem appropriate – he was a bit of a showman himself who once a year hosted a grand party with a band and cabaret acts. There's a story that at one point during the war when parts were in scarce supply Evelyn would go to visit his shop, leave her handbag open on the counter and whisper to one of the mechanics to slip in a few frame lugs while she took Claud out for a drink.

Evelyn sold her own bikes, from her shop on Streatham High Road. © Micky Bannon

Who was she really? We like to say 'truth is stranger than fiction', but sometimes the myths are so much better than reality. That's particularly true in cycling, and the 'Technicolor' version of Evelyn's life story is a gift to a spy novelists, or Hollywood. Perhaps the most paradoxical thing about all this is that thanks to those archive films, she appears to be the most 'real' of the riders of her era.

51 Evelyn Hamilton

MARGUERITE WILSON

'The Blonde Bombshell'

In 1935 Ethel Rolf packed some sandwiches and set off on her bike from her home near Guildford, to ride 75 miles to Bournemouth. The plan was to take part in the Bournemouth Arrow's Ladies' 10-mile time trial the following day. Women's races were hard to come by in the mid 1930s, just as it was hard to find clubs that admitted women. In 1934 Ethel had tried taking part in some men's events, only to get her knuckles rapped by the Road Records Association, which didn't allow women to race with men.

So the 75-mile journey for an opportunity to race was well worth the effort, even if it did mean Ethel had the awkward task of carrying her 'sprints' – a spare set of wheels with lightweight wooden rims for racing – while she rode. She stayed the night in a cycle shop near the course that also operated as a B&B. Supper was fish and chips. That evening Ethel got chatting with the shop owner's daughter, who told her about a 17-year old local girl called Marguerite Wilson who would very probably win the race. She knew her well, because they trained in the same gym. 'There was no mistaking her at the start – all blonde hair and bronzed legs', Ethel later recalled. Marguerite won the race as predicted, despite having never ridden a time trial, with a bike, nicknamed 'old crock', that was more like a touring bike with its heavy steel wheels. Ethel came second. And for the next few years, that was how things would continue.

Marguerite was so prodigiously strong that the best riders usually resigned themselves to a fight for second place when they saw her name on the start sheet. Ethel and Marguerite became great friends. They were part of a generation of remarkable women, starting with the founders of the Rosslyn Ladies CC in 1922, who transformed cycling culture in Britain, making it one of the most inclusive countries in the world for the women's sport. They wrote articles in cycling magazines, they criss-crossed the country to get to races, and they rode with such determination and talent that they earned men's admiration along the way. They paved the way for the likes of Eileen Sheridan, Millie Robinson, Beryl Burton and many others.

Ethel, who later took her husband's surname Brambleby, ended up riding for 68 years, during which time she established four women's records and completed 40 12-hour time trials. She was a founding member of the Women's Road Record Association (WRRA), which was created in 1934 in response to the RRA refusing to sanction women's record attempts.

Marguerite seemed to win everything with apparently little more calculation than simply turning up in time for the start. 'She would think nothing of riding from Bournemouth to Bedford (135 miles) and back to the Isle of Wight – always carrying camping kit', Ethel later recalled. In 1939 she was hired by Hercules – at that time the biggest bike manufacturer in the world – to break the 16 records outlined in the WRRA book.

She broke 11 of them in the course of six months, her inexorable progress only brought to a halt by the outbreak of the Second World War. She finished off the job with a new sponsor, Claud Butler, in 1940, when she was only 22. In 1941 she and another rider, Ann Briercliffe, were the first to ride 50 miles in under two hours. 'It was poetry in motion to see her riding powerfully along the road, with her tanned legs spinning, a radiant smile and blonde hair flowing in the breeze', Ethel recalled. 'She certainly sold cycling for Hercules, for she was one of the most attractive girls ever to ride a bike and was idolised by the lads.'

Marguerite Wilson was born near Poole Harbour in Dorset, in 1918. She attended a local school for promising young children with the potential to become teachers. She excelled in sport, and became a member of the netball, hockey and tennis teams, with which she travelled all over the South of England. She was also a natural in athletics, winning County medals for running and hurdling and winning the school's all-round sports medal four years in a row.

'My whole being centred around sport and athletics', she later wrote, 'and I firmly resolved that were it at all possible, I was going to make a name for myself in the sporting sphere'. More precisely, she dreamt of becoming an Olympic champion in the mould of her heroine, the American 'Babe' Zaharias, who had won two gold medals at the 1932 Olympics: 'With this in view, I set out to try to start an athletic club for ladies in my home town, Bournemouth, where no such club existed.' She found, however, 'that the male members of various local athletics clubs resented the intrusion of women into their pastime', while other female athletes 'were only half-hearted in their efforts when they knew they had not the support of the males.' Marguerite tried other things. She took up weight training, and played hockey at weekends. She tried tennis, swimming and even skating. She'd been invited by a local boy with a tandem to take part in some rides with the local Bournemouth Arrow CC, which she 'really hated', but she nonetheless joined the club. Then she got her own lightweight bike and things changed.

'I learned the real joys of cycling, the benefits of healthy surroundings and company, and the smell of the open road and freedom, which, in spite of my love of sport I had never really experienced before. Every club run was an adventure, an exploration, taking me to places where I had never been before.' Cycling was not just a sport, but also a social scene. On Sunday club runs everyone – the slow group and the fast – would meet at a designated time for tea. There was an annual party in January and throughout the winter there were club nights offering 'dancing and sociability'.

The club also published a quarterly magazine called *The Reflector*, which featured arch accounts of madcap jaunts to races. Marguerite's account of taking part in the North-Western Ladies '25' held outside London, along with two other club-mates with whom she formed a women's team, is particularly entertaining. The plan was to ride up to Southampton on the Saturday afternoon before the race, where a friend with a Morris two-seater would give the four of them (three girls and one fiancé) a lift to London. When they reached Southhampton, they discovered their friend was no longer able to offer the promised lift. 'I tentatively suggested that he might consent to let me drive everybody', Marguerite wrote. 'His answer was a most emphatic "no" at first, but after much persuasion he reluctantly consented to let me drive.'

The gang's naivety in matters of car maintenance meant they promptly ran out of petrol, adding further delay to their progress and they received some funny looks along the way. 'No wonder people stared – three girls in shorts, looking like school-kids, crowded into the front seat, and one fellow, sitting all alone in the dickey [a fold-out seat in the boot of pre-war cars] with bicycles draped all around him! We had to sling one machine over the bonnet of the car, having no room elsewhere for it; and this, of course, impeded my vision to no little extent.' They eventually reached their final destination – at 2.30am. Unable to sleep in the car, they talked until dawn, breakfasted on apples and bananas and waited for the race to start – which Marguerite then won, while the girls' combined efforts secured the team prize.

'I really believe that the thought of celebrating afterwards made us try more in races than the actual competition,' she later wrote, 'and I speak for all of us when I say, contrary to most people who race, we really *did* enjoy our racing.'

In 1937 she signed up for her first ever 12-hour time trial, organised by the Rosslyn Ladies. She had never ridden anything like this distance, but felt compelled to have a go, 'mostly because all the lads in the club said I may be good at "25s", and almost equal their times, but at least it took a man to ride a "12". This rather got my goat, so, unknown to anybody, I entered.' After receiving her start card, she admitted to being, "rather scared" – she had never raced more than 25 miles – and 'wondered whether I hadn't let my pride take me a little too far.' Despite at 18 being one of the youngest entrants, she won the race with a distance of 209 miles and would have even set a course record if she hadn't been misdirected at one point by a course marshal. 'Such was the club spirit among the girls in those pre-war days', Ethel later

'The thought of celebrating afterwards made us try more in races than the actual competition.'

recalled, 'that, on the occasion of the 12-hour, two of Marguerite's club-mates [Ruth Merchant and Frances Morris] left Bournemouth at 4 o'clock Saturday afternoon and rode through the night across London to reach Epping [120 miles away] by the start of the event and then helped her throughout the day before returning home again.'

The following year Marguerite won the 12-hour again, this time setting a course record with 215 miles and 296 yards. However, this was 'no real indication of her sterling ride', as Ethel later explained. 'She had one burst tyre, and subsequent deflations through riding bald tyres. At one stage an inner tube was showing through the tread, and she rode a detour on a borrowed bike while a helper changed a tyre from his bike to hers!' By the end of the 1938 season her career palmarès featured 25 races, of which she had lost only three, and a number of distance records, including an improvement on the 196-miles London–York record by more an half an hour, stiff winds notwithstanding, and 100 mile records both alone and on an all-female tandem. The 'Blonde Bombshell' (as the press dubbed her) and her devastating rides did not go unnoticed. One person paying particular attention was Frank Southall, the racing manager for The Hercules Cycle and Motor Company. Southall was an Olympic medallist, who had broken nine place-to-place records and won the British Best All Rounder award between 1930 and 1933. He considered Marguerite, 'the most amazing proposition on two wheels'. So in 1939 she became the first woman on Hercules' all-male team tasked with breaking endurance and place-to-place records. With her two British and three Belgian teammates, she was one of only 13 professional riders in the whole country. The Hercules riders were set up in a hotel in Kingston-upon-Thames from which they did 50-mile 'time trials' every morning, followed by doing strength training in the gym in the afternoons.

Marguerite didn't just break records, she smashed them, at regular intervals. She improved her previous London to York record by 50 minutes and after a two-minute pause forged on to set a staggering new 12-hour record of 230 miles. She did this having eaten only one sandwich and a banana. One of the helpers, Tommy Hall, a former record breaker himself, described her performance as, 'the most phenomenal ride I have ever seen.'

A week later she took 13m 31s off the London to Brighton record, and a few weeks after that she was riding the 212 miles from Edinburgh to Liverpool. She set out without breakfast, having accidentally overslept. The road-side helpers had all gone home, assuming she'd either abandoned or not started. In the support car behind, 'half a crown' was mustered with which some cakes, biscuits and bottles of lemonade were bought to sustain her until she reached Liverpool, where she set a new record, despite being docked 26-minutes for the late start. Later in May she took the record for London to Portsmouth and back by 53 minutes, then in July took the 210-mile London–Bath record. During the ride she caught and passed men competing on the Bath Road 100-mile time trial. Only three men had ever ridden faster than her, one of whom was her teammate Richard Kemps, who considered it one of the hardest rides he'd ever done.

Cycling Magazine reported: 'Miss Wilson rode throughout like a machine, covering 22 miles in both the first and last hour, never dismounted and seemed exceptionally fresh at the finish.' In July she took on the daunting 287 miles from Land's End to London. Riding up through Cornwall she encountered strong side winds and rain followed by thick mist on Bodmin moor. She reached Hyde Park Corner at 5am, looking remarkably fresh, despite having ridden for just over 17 hours. Ten minutes later she set off again in pursuit of the 24-hour record, riding into East Anglia where she reached Wymondham at 12 noon with a distance of 396 miles. Epic though this ride was, it was only a warm-up for the most mythic of British place-to-place records; Land's End to John o' Groats, in which riders trace the 870 miles separating the two most distant points on the British mainland. Only one woman had ridden it before: Lilian Dredge, a founding member of the WRRA. Her record stood at 3 days, 20 hours and 54 minutes. She had carried on to establish a 1,000-mile record in 4 days, 19 hours and 14 minutes. Record attempts are usually only done in optimal conditions, ideally with a tail wind. Marguerite could not afford to wait – it was the end of August, already late in the year given what the weather could do in the Scottish mountains. More significantly, there was also the possibility Britain might declare war against Germany at any moment, which would probably mean having to cancel the attempt. Marguerite therefore set off directly into a headwind, an act of madness under normal circumstances. By the time she had reached Bodmin Moor, 56 miles later and dramatically behind schedule, her team suggested she abandon.

A publicity shot from 1939, taken for one of the Hercules team sponsors. © Beverley Aldeslade Collection

But Marguerite remained calm. She understood it was now or never. Her schedule allowed for considerable slowing down towards the end of the ride and she thought she might make up for lost time later. She plugged on, stopping in a Devon village for a cup of tea, taking half an hour's rest at Bristol and an hour at Worcester, where she had a nap in the caravan that was following her. She rode into the night, gradually clawing back lost time. She passed through Shropshire at dawn, then worked her way across the Cheshire plains into Lancashire, through the industrial towns of Wigan, Preston and Lancaster and up into Cumbria where she climbed Shap Fell. She reached Carlisle 10 minutes

up on her schedule and rested for three hours. At 6pm she reached the Scottish border, having covered 480 miles.

'The main thing for me to do was to try and keep cheerful, and not worry unduly about the ride I had in front of me', she later said. She focussed on 'things I would do when the ride was over, and the fact that by the time I had finished, pay day would be round again!'. In Scotland the climbing began in earnest, going through Moffat, up the Devil's Beef Tub, then up through Stirling and Perth before crossing the Cairngorms. It was here that she finished clawing back the three hours on the schedule that she'd lost resting in Carlisle.

She actually looked forward to the long Scottish climbs, 'because I soon learned that it was always at the top of these that I would find a little band of helpers waiting to encourage me, while a good free-wheel for my efforts rewarded me down the other side.'

Marguerite enjoyed certain luxuries – she was followed by a caravan where she could take naps where necessary, and she had a chef who cooked meals for her. But how each individual responds to such gruelling effort varies from one rider to the next. 'Sleepiness did not trouble me nearly as much as loneliness', she later wrote, 'After all, you can imagine a girl (and an especially talkative one at that!) going for three whole days and nights without hardly speaking to a soul! However, I fully made up for it when I did stop, because of the 10½ hours that I spent out of the saddle, only 3½ were taken up by sleeping.'

Demonstration race, International Six Day, Wembley, June 1939. © Beverley Aldeslade Collection

She had a terrifying moment going over the Aultnamain mountain beyond Inverness. 'In the pitch-blackness of the night, and after two days' riding I found it absolutely treacherous, and I count myself very lucky indeed that I had no serious accident', she later recalled. 'More than once instinct seemed to warn me I was near danger, and I would jam on the brakes as the cycle sped down a mountainside only to find myself overlooking a sheer drop over the edge where I should have gone round a hairpin bend.'

From Bonar Bridge she moved back to the coast road for the remaining 90 or so hilly miles, whistling to herself whenever she felt tired or lonely. She finally reached John o' Groats at 8.52am, having completed the ride roughly a day faster than Dredge in 2 days, 22 hours and 52 minutes.

After a bath, a change of clothes and a good meal she set out again for a further 130 miles to attack the 1,000-mile record. As she rode, Britain declared war on Germany. Marguerite, being on the road, was quite unaware of this and was startled to reach Wick, her final destination, in utter darkness because of the blackout. She had covered the 1,000 miles in 3 days, 11 hours and 44 minutes, improving Dredge's record by one day and 7½ hours.

The following February she became the first woman to win the prestigious F.T. Bidlake Memorial Prize, given each year to the person who has made the greatest contribution to cycling.

'It is clear that not a vestige of the ancient prejudice against fast and long-distance cycling by women survives,' wrote the *CTC* (Cyclists' Touring Club) *Gazette*'s popular female columnist 'Petronella', who was actually Evelyn Parkes, the WRRA's president. Her husband, G.H. Stancer, was the chairman of the prize.

More tea... with friends from the Bournemouth Arrow cc. © William Wilson collection

War brought Marguerite's record-breaking campaign with Hercules to an end, but in 1940 she was employed by the London manufacturer Claud Butler, for whom she set further records. These were harder to obtain since wartime precautions meant there were no weather forecasts and all the road signs were taken down. Marguerite nonetheless broke a further seven records.

Marguerite volunteered as an ambulance driver, and in 1942 started working for BOAC (the British Overseas Airways Corporation), starting out as a stewardess and becoming a traffic officer for their fleet of flying boats in Poole Harbour, Hythe and Southampton. Though NCU rules meant she could no longer race, and there were no more records to break, Pathé films from 1945 and 1948 show her still riding her bike, taking part in a 'roller racing evening' and riding on the track after a day's work at BOAC.

After the war she married a test pilot called Ron Stone and for a brief period they lived in Canada, where she soon joined a local club and took part in their training runs, much to the consternation of some of its (all male) members. 'They were astonished that I not only managed to hang on to them, but had a go at the front myself when the occasion demanded', she recalled.

During this period she took part in three men's amateur road races. Despite having no experience of bunch riding, crashing near the start and losing ten minutes due to broken spokes, she finished her first race in 5th place. A four-man break crossed the finish line first, but Marguerite was the best sprinter in the peloton behind. With similar mishaps she came 9th in her second race, which was 100 miles long, and 7th in her third. One can only wonder what sort of a road cyclist she might have become, had she been born in another era. Sadly a bad back injury requiring spinal surgery forced to give up the bike for good in 1949. Back in England she took up golfing, at which she proved to have another great talent, and had a daughter who also took up the sport, playing at national and county level.

She died tragically young, at the age of only 54, in 1972. Her cause of death was never officially given, and William Wilson, whose father was her cousin, provides no clues in the biography he has lovingly compiled on her. Yet in cycling circles it was known that she'd taken her life.

Can you have too much happiness too early in life, so that nothing later measures up? Did all those accounts of jolly adventures hide a personality that periodically stared into the abyss? Was it already there, behind those courageous and determined rides? Marguerite's career presents so many what ifs: what if there'd been a women's world championships or Olympics during her lifetime? What if there hadn't been the WRRA and the goals it provided women to aim for? What if she'd been allowed to continue racing?

Repairing 'Old Crock' Westerham Railway Station, Kent, 1938. © William Wilson collection

Marguerite Wilson put women's cycling on the map in Britain. She became a figurehead who inspired a generation of women and men to take up the sport, putting the more conservative elements of the cycling establishment on notice: things would no longer be the same.

'The Wheeling Sheilas'

In 1925, members of the Sale Cycle Club were debating whether they should hold a women's road race. 'The cyclists fought the matter down to the confinement (should this event take place) of a distance not greater than three miles, and no lady allowed to ride a gent's cycle,' reported the *Gippsland Times*.

Someone suggested inviting members of the Ladies Rowing Club, since they probably wouldn't have enough female cyclists. Hubert Opperman, the previous year's national champion, told the paper he would 'journey from Melbourne to see such an event take place.' At that point, no one could possibly have predicted that within a few years Opperman would become 'Oppy', a folk hero who had had ridden the Tour de France and won two of the hardest races in the European cycling calendar.

Even less could they have imagined that within the same timeframe, a full peloton's worth of feisty young women would be criss-crossing the continent, setting and breaking records over hundreds of miles with dazzling chutzpah. By the time they had finished making their point, discussions of whether they should be allowed to do a three mile race on proper racing bikes would be quite redundant. As it turned out, the women's and Opperman's stories were inextricably linked.

If any country appreciated the invention of the bicycle, it was Australia. Throughout the 19th century and into the 20th, Australians got around their vast continent with horses, donkeys and camels, or by taking ships along the coast. Train lines were scant, and it wasn't until 1917 that there was a transcontinental service. The safety bicycle, introduced at the end of the 1880s, proved a godsend for Australia's rural workers such as the gold prospectors, sheep-shearers and telegraph maintenance workers who routinely needed to cover great distances. It could handle dusty tracks and uneven surfaces, could carry swag bags or transport mail, didn't require food and water, and most importantly, was much faster than any other means of transport in the absence of trains.

While the bike was great, cycling conditions were not. 'There were no sealed roads at all for some 80% of the continent, well into the 1980s', points out Jim Fitzpatrick, the author of *Wheeling Matilda: The Story of Australian Cycling*. Settlements were far and few between. With temperatures capable of rising up to 50°C in the arid, oven-hot interior, you only had to make one simple mistake, like going off track or running out of water, and your goose was cooked. And if the elements didn't do you in, then there was always the possibility of a run-in with the wildlife. Those rural cyclists were the sort of mythic figures who became central to Australia's developing identity as a land of can-do pioneers, and Australians were quick to appreciate the endurance feats of great riders who seemed to be cut from the same cloth.

They didn't have to be men. Take the case of Miss Lucy Beyer, a, 'young, tall, fair, remarkably pretty, and a splendid type of a healthy Australian girl,' who in 1896 rode the 568.8 miles between Sydney and Melbourne in seven and a half days – about 76 miles a day. Sponsored by the maker of the 'Myee rational skirt' ('wind powerless to raise') she encountered rain, mud, heat, headwinds and dust. One day she suffered 8 punctures, another day she had to cycle with only one leg for ten miles because of a broken pedal. Late one evening her chain broke, and she had to walk 14 miles to the nearest settlement. On yet another occasion she lost a shoe. She was held up by her brother, who was accompanying her and fell ill.

When asked if she had 'suffered any fatigue' she replied, 'Oh, dear no! Not the slightest. I arrived in Melbourne as fresh as possible, and feeling as well as ever I did in my life, nor have I suffered any inconvenience since. Indeed, I am sure I could have ridden for another week without being tired.' A month later Mrs Newton covered the distance in 6 days and 13 hours, despite having to 'slow down repeatedly and wait for her husband.'

In 1898 Mrs H. P. Nicolls covered the route in 6 days and 7 hours, despite her chain breaking twice. She did this through 'high winds and heavy rainstorms', on tracks that were 'narrow sheets of water and slush.' Nicolls, it turned out, was the sister of F. T. Bidlake, the founder of the Road Records Association in Britain who essentially invented time-trialling as we know it today. Bidlake didn't like women racing and thought 'rational dress' was 'laughable.' Did he know that his sister, on the other side of the world, was busy breaking records in knickerbockers?

At the same time as Lucy Beyer's ride, the *Australian town and Country Journal*, reported that in Western Australia, 'Miss O'Meagher, a Menzies cycliste, thinks nothing of riding between that town and Coolgardie. The other day she covered the journey – a little over 90 miles – in about nine hours, and attended a ball in the evening.'

> 'The other day she covered the journey – a little over 90 miles – in about nine hours, and attended a ball in the evening.'

What happened to these amazing women with their Wild West swagger? After about 1900 news of them and their rides peters out. Cycling, for women at least, seems to have gone out of fashion – for 30 years. Why this should be is hard to fathom. Could it have been the arrival of cars? Or a recovery from the global recession of the 1890s, and a corresponding increase in wealth which 'allowed' them to lead more 'ladylike' lives?

In 1929 the shockwaves of the Wall Street Crash hit Australia and the certainties and social mores of previous decades were turned on their head. By 1932 unemployment had reached a record high of 30%. The trauma and economic hardship suffered by Australians was far worse than that experienced in any other industrialised nation other than Germany. Many Australians became utterly destitute, reduced to living in shacks and begging on the streets. War heroes lost their homes. Suicide rates shot up.

Out of this period of desolation emerged a number of extraordinary sporting heroes, like the cricketer Don Bradman and the racehorse Phar Lap, whose achievements remain legendary even today. They distracted people from their day-to-day suffering and gave them a renewed feeling of pride in what it meant to be Australian. Hubert Opperman was one of these great figures: he wasn't just a remarkable athlete, but a courageous one who excelled in the most daunting of challenges.

He led the first Australian team to ride the Tour de France. They were woefully outnumbered by much bigger and wealthier European teams. Opperman rode most of it on his own when his teammates couldn't keep up. He won the famous Bol d'Or 24-hour track race in Paris, despite the fact that both his bikes had been sabotaged. He won the 1,200km endurance epic, Paris–Brest–Paris, setting a new course record, and he broke numerous place-to-place records in Britain, including the most difficult, Land's End to John o' Groats. He rode for 24 hours behind a motorbike on the track and managed to cover more than 860 miles. And all this was merely an aperitif for his pièce de résistance on home turf: an epic 2,875 mile Fremantle–Sydney transcontinental ride which took five days off the previous record.

While Opperman was on the boat to Europe for his second Tour de France in 1931, two friends, Phyllis Sharman and Melba White, decided to ride the 607 miles from Adelaide to Melbourne. They did it in about ten days, of which three had been spent resting. They arrived in Melbourne 'looking very tired', reported *The Horsham Times*. 'Miss Sharman stated on arrival that the journey was undertaken for a joke, but they would not have tried it if they had known how hard it was.'

A few weeks later two other friends, Mrs M Cameron and Miss May McEntee, did the same ride again, but in nearly half the time (5 days and 9 hours). In June, 19-year old Doreen Middleton rode the other way in 4 days and 21 hours. A few weeks later she rode back, this time in four days, despite having to dodge wild rabbits and a kangaroo in the Coorong desert. She had allowed herself only 18 hours' sleep. A crowd of 5,000 greeted her in Melbourne where she was hoisted onto the top of her father's car and driven through the streets in triumph. The distance-devouring ladies were back, and they meant business.

Middleton was a model for those who would come in her wake. The daughter of a racing cyclist, she had been training since March and had found a sponsor, Navy Cycles, who provided her with a racing frame and wheels. She had enlisted officials from two regional cycling unions to monitor her attempt to be absolutely sure her ride was independently witnessed and ratified. There was no doubt: this one was for the record books.

Doreen Middleton (last rider). © Dawn Trowell Collection

The following year it was the turn of 20-year old Elsa Barbour to make headlines by riding 565 miles from Sydney to Melbourne in 3 days, 7 hours and 25 minutes. On the last day she rode 154 miles, mostly into a headwind. She'd only been riding for a year and had taken up the sport on her doctor's advice after badly scalding her legs. Despite her relative inexperience, she'd already set several records racing on the track, and was also sponsored by Navy Cycles. There to congratulate her on her arrival in Melbourne was Doreen.

Her ride was not without controversy. While it had been carefully monitored by an official from the New South Wales Amateur Cyclists' Union, the Victorian Amateur Cyclists Union (or VACU) refused to ratify it and even issued her with a fine, since she had also broken the women's half-mile record on the Sydney track without their permission. In the midst of the brouhaha the Amateur Cyclists Association of Australia (ACAA) weighed in, pointing out that its constitution and rules didn't include women, and therefore, 'no records in events run for women shall be recognised.'

No matter: the following year Barbour went after Middleton's Adelaide to Melbourne record, reducing it by a full 24 hours, covering the 607 miles in a staggering 2 days, 23 hours and 17 minutes.

In May 1934 a 23 year old working at the Melbourne *Argus* newspaper decided to have a crack at Barbour's Sydney–Melbourne record, but in the opposite direction. At 4ft 11 and weighing 45 kilos, Billie Samuel was barely larger than the koala teddy bear mascot she strapped to her handlebars. She had only been riding a bike for four months but she didn't let this hold her back. There'd been a heated debate in the office about whether ordinary women were really capable of these endurance rides, and she felt she had to make a point. If she could do it, so could any woman.

She was sponsored by Bruce Small, a local businessman who owned a bike shop called Malvern Star. Small had also been sponsoring Opperman since 1921 and in the process the two men had become firm friends and business collaborators. Small arranged for Samuel to be coached by Ossie Nicholson, Opperman's Tour de France teammate and another Malvern Star rider. The previous year Ossie had set a world record for the greatest distance ridden in one year, and had done the Sydney–Melbourne ride himself in four days. Billie spent 8 weeks training intensively under his direction. She would do the ride alone, taking a

Below: Billie rode the 565 miles in 3 days, 1 hr, 25 mins. © State Library of New South Wales

logbook which she had stamped by 'leading citizens' in post offices along the way, since the VACU had by now clarified that it didn't recognise women's records.

She set out from Melbourne at 5am on her 3-speed Malvern Star Bike and arrived in Wangaratta 150 miles later at 8.40pm, exhausted and bruised having come off her bike. The next day she fell behind schedule with a second crash forcing her to make emergency repairs. Encountering difficult cycling conditions, she rode into the night, pulling over at 2am to take a nap by the roadside. She slept longer than intended, and by the time she reached Gundagai the next morning she was more than 12 hours behind schedule. She didn't reach Sydney General Post Office, her final destination, until after 11pm, where her anxious parents were waiting for her: the first thing her father had known about her project was when he read about it in the papers. She had failed to crack Barbour's time, completing her ride in three days, 17 hours and two minutes, but had at least claimed a record as the first woman to ride the other way.

Joyce Barry helps promote the Milk Board. © State Library of New South Wales

Six weeks later she rode back. By then it was early July and deep into the Australian winter. She had to contend with heavy rain and mud and was obliged to carry her bike on certain stretches. More crashes and injuries ensued, but this time she had periods with the wind at her back, and she rode into Melbourne in triumph, breaking Barbour's record by more than six hours. More than 3,000 spectators came out to greet her. Overcome with emotion, she burst into tears.

Bike manufacturing was one of the few industries that flourished during the recession and Bruce Small's business was rapidly expanding thanks, amongst other things, to a new company he'd set up that offered loans with which to buy his bikes. In 1937 Small found the female equivalent of 'Oppy' and quickly put her on the payroll. Joyce Barry was a photogenic

18 year-old typist from Sydney and a natural athlete, who excelled in running, high jumping, skating, hiking, rifle shooting and dancing. She had several years' riding in her legs, having been encouraged by her doctor to take up cycling after getting pneumonia when she was 15. She was 5ft 11 with wavy blond hair and mesmerisingly long legs.

'Cycling on my Malvern Star in the fresh open air keeps me slim and ensures that delightful bloom which no cosmetic could impart', she (or the Malvern Star copywriter) declared in one advert. In her striking yellow jersey and black shorts, she soon earned the nickname 'The Flying Wasp.'

Opperman took her under his wing, helping her train for the speed and endurance records Small wanted her to obtain. They seemed inseparable, and people soon started calling her 'Miss Oppie.' Barry was clearly a great talent, with a powerful sprint that helped her win many track races, but it was her ambitious long distance place-to-place rides that made her the Alpha girl of distance records. She dispatched Samuel's Sydney–Melbourne record, bettering it by 22 hours. She rode faster than the midnight express train in Western Australia, where she covered the 116 miles from Bunbury to Perth in 6 hours and 15 minutes. She broke a man's record: the 483.9 mile 'villainous course' of Brisbane–Rockhampton, improving on Bill Withers' time, set only two years previously, with a margin of 22 hours and 56 minutes.

But while the press consistently reported Barry's many triumphs, they also relished those of her increasingly competitive rivals, such as 16-year-old Jean Sexton who beat Barry's Orange–Sydney record by 9 minutes, or Valda Unthank, who broke Barry's 50-mile unpaced road record, or Miss Irene Pyle, who ran a dress shop in Wangaratta, and pulverised Barry's Melbourne–Sydney record by covering the distance in 1 day, 16 hours and 23 minutes, nearly ten and a half hours faster than Barry. She had been a spectator in Wangaratta five years previously when Billie had set her record, and had been inspired to take up cycling as a result.

In a country as vast as Australia, of course, there was no end of new challenges to invent, with regional records almost as prestigious as national ones. With bike manufacturers like Malvern Star, Healing, Speedwell and Navy Cycles pursuing new records and providing sponsorship, there was also no shortage of ambitious women keen to have a go, resulting in a women's cycling boom whose only comparable precedent might be the women's track racing scene in North America of the 1890s.

It was no longer enough just to do a plucky ride in adverse weather conditions over great distances. What the sponsors wanted now was records, and to keep 'em coming. Once every few weeks would be nice. Bruce Small planned

a demanding programme for Joyce in 1939. In addition to taking back many of her records, she would become the first woman to see how far she could get by riding for seven days non-stop. Ossie Nicholson would be her coach, having set a seven day record himself in 1938 with 1,507½ miles. No woman had ever attempted such madness.

By this point Malvern Star had expanded from a single shop in 1920 to the leading bike brand in Australia, with 24 stores and 450 agencies across the country. They could afford to do things in style, supplying Barry with a full support team and a luxury caravan for when she needed to take naps.

So on 4 September 1939, three days after the start of the Second World War, Barry set out for a week's non-stop riding. She set herself an objective of 1000 miles and chose to ride on a 35-mile course that circled around Sydney and its suburbs.

Joyce Barry's figures 'bid fair to remain for a considerable period', reported the *Daily Mercury* on the sixth day of her ride, while praising her 'extraordinarily good form'. So it must have been with great relief, at the end of seven days and a mind-numbing 31 laps, that Barry successfully re-established her Alpha status, with a distance of 1,107 miles. Alas, her record only lasted two months.

In November the new star Valda Unthank smashed Barry's seven day record in crushing style, covering a distance of 1,438.4 miles. In the first 24 hours alone she rode 235.5 miles, despite encountering wind and rain. 'What a ride! Mere man takes off his hat to Valda Unthank!' declared Melbourne's *Sporting Globe*.

Unthank had been sponsored by Austral Cycles, another company in Bruce Small's expanding portfolio, and had a full support crew, with 'Oppie' driving the car that accompanied her and Ossie helping to keep her awake during the long and lonely hours of the night by singing songs like 'Boomps–a–Daisy' and 'The Lambeth Walk.' Spectators turned out in droves to watch her. In one photo you can see her sitting in a showroom eating her lunch with Ossie. The pavement outside is crowded with onlookers, their noses glued to the window.

The record breaking came to a climax four months later when Pat Hawkins, an 18-year old rider from Western Australia with little over a year's riding experience, smashed both Valda and Ossie's seven day records, with a distance of 1,546 miles.

Like so many riders, Hawkins seemed to have come out of nowhere. She had first been spotted by a representative of Bruce Small Pty Ltd out in Western Australia who happened to drive past her while she was out on her bike. He signed her to Malvern Star on the spot. For her seven day record she was followed by a car kitted with something called a Philips Portaphone, a sort of

Right: Just like the male pros, Joyce Barry signed postcards for her fans. © State Library of New South Wales

radio with a microphone. Whenever she appeared to be flagging, someone in the car would sing her a special ditty, to the tune of 'Daisy Bell':

> 'Patsy, Patsy, teach me to ride like you.
> We're all crazy over the rides you do
> No wonder the crowd's astounded
> And you are always surrounded
> By an admiring throng
> As you pedal along
> On a Malvern Star built for You.'

Pat liked music but I can imagine this must have grated after a while. In 1939 the papers had reported with great interest on her Perth–York record, in which she'd had a jazz saxophonist playing to her in the first of three accompanying cars.

As she completed her ride 'looking as fresh as a daisy', huge crowds thronged the streets to greet her and she was inundated with bouquets of flowers.

Valda must have been bitterly disappointed, yet managed a terse message of congratulations. There was silence from Ossie. Only Oppy, it seemed, felt sufficiently unthreatened to be fulsome in his praise.

Early in the week he had sent Hawkins a telegram:
> 'Pat—Nice work to date—it will get tough towards the end—but everyone feels that way—just remember there's plenty of time to rest afterwards and the more tired you are the better you enjoy the stop.—Cheerio and best of luck.' When, in the course of her ride she broke the 1,000 mile record he sent another one: 'Your performance leaves me gasping; thought Valda's 1,438 miles would last indefinitely. Accept hearty pack on the back for every mile. Oppy.'

What else was there left to do? So many records had been broken, reporters were getting nonchalant. So, for example, in September 1940, *The Evening News* in

Rockhampton informed readers that Miss Jean Pengilly 'broke seven Western Australian, two Australian cycling records and two world records established by Marguerite Wilson, of England'. The records were for 50 miles, which Pengilly covered in 2 hours and 50 seconds, and for 100 miles, which she covered in 4 hours, 13 minutes and 50 seconds. 'After finishing her ride at 10am she had a bath and went to work,' the paper added.

There'd been some fighting talk from Valda about taking her seven day record back, but soon afterwards she announced she was putting cycling on hold to focus on the war effort. After her seven day record in 1939, Barry's name disappears from newspaper reports. Had she been dropped by Small, after being eclipsed by Unthank and Hawkins? Perhaps she was quietly relieved.

The only rider who seemed to keep going was Hawkins, who in February 1941 set out to break a record set in England by Billie Dovey for the greatest distance ridden in a year. By October she'd already passed Dovey's record, despite the fact that her mother had died, leaving her to look after her 10 siblings (every morning she prepared packed lunches for all of them before going on her rides). She'd also lost seven weeks to illness and injury. She continued riding until February 1942, regularly clocking 900-mile weeks, to make it a full 12 months, 45,000 miles to Dovey's 29,000. Not only that, but also she broke Ossie Nicholson's record of 43,996¾ miles established in 1937. Yet only a week later, officials refused to ratify the record, having found 'certain irregularities in Miss Hawkin's log sheets.' Malvern Cycles quickly distanced themselves from the scandal and the record breaking era seemed to come to an end.

What's particularly remarkable, sifting through the newspaper archives, is how much these women's achievements were celebrated. Of course, financial interests were also at stake and sponsoring attractive female riders was clearly a smart marketing move. When entire newspaper pages were dedicated to celebrating a female rider's achievements, they were also crammed with related sponsors' adverts. After Hawkins' seven day ride, you might find two thirds of the page in a newspaper taken up with adverts from her sponsors, like Malvern Star who provided the bike, Pontiac who provided a support car, Peters Ice Cream who provided snacks, The Health and Beauty Clinic Ltd who provided massages, Judith Aden Lotions, 'the ideal skin preservers for the outdoor girl', Philips portable radios, Leggett's tyres and the Cyclo 4-speed gear system.

After the war, a new generation of young riders emerged, who also raced on the road. Iris Dixon (née Bent) was one of that generation's stars, and is still alive and riding today, a member of the 'Golden Oldies' club outside Melbourne. Her speciality was track racing, and she was a phenomenal talent. But she told me there was never any question that she would want to undertake such gruelling endurance records as her predecessors. That era had become a thing of the past.

By 1955, Australian women's racing had disappeared again, just as inexplicably as in the early years of the 20th century. 'Oppy' went on to become a successful politician and received an OBE in 1952. Bruce Small sold Malvern Cycles in 1958, the same year the company reported its biggest ever sales of £2 million. At its peak after the war, the business had 115 stores with 1,000 dealers. He went into politics and property development, and became mayor of the Gold Coast where he was celebrated for introducing 'Meter Maids' – young women clad in gold bikinis who feed parking meters – as a way of promoting the Surfer's Paradise beach resort.

> When entire newspaper pages were dedicated to celebrating a female rider's achievements, they were also crammed with related sponsors' adverts.

And the women just went back to their jobs as secretaries or sales assistants, or they got married and caught up in domestic life.

EILEEN SHERIDAN

'The Mighty Atom'

Eileen Sheridan was the poster girl for post-war British pluck. She was immensely talented, determined and courageous while at the same time eternally cheery. You only have to look at pictures of her pedalling in the rain, hands down on the drops, gobbling up the road at a tidy lick, a big goofy grin on her face, to feel an urgent need to get on the bike yourself.

Life might be tough, work and food scarce, she seemed to say, but if you go for a good spin in the fresh air, you'll be all the fitter and happier for it.

She would go out and set records over huge distances at a pace that would put most men to shame, and yet she radiated such good will that no rider could be jealous of her overtaking them or breaking their records. All they could do was applaud her outstanding talent. Where her great predecessor, Marguerite Wilson, was the sort of powerful-looking athlete Leni Riefenstahl's camera would have locked onto, had women's cycling been an Olympic sport, Eileen, at just under five foot, was quite the opposite; a dimpled, bird-like brunette, everyone's common-or-garden sweetheart, as fresh and uncomplicated as a forget-me-not. And with her skimpy black shorts, she was just a little bit sassy too.

The Hercules Cycle and Motor Company wanted to bottle and sell some of that Sheridan joie-de-vivre. They paid her royally; on the back of her three-year contract with them she was able to buy a car and a house had a degree of financial security that would have been quite unimaginable for a female rider in the UK, or anywhere else for that matter. Even today, such money is a fantasy for most professional female riders. Perhaps just as remarkable was the fact that Eileen was only the second British rider to be offered a professional contract in postwar Britain, the first going to the great track specialist and multiple world champion, Reg Harris.

Eileen's sponsors certainly got a good return on their investment. In the space of three years, between 1952 and 1954, she broke all the existing 21 distance and place-to-place records, from 25 miles to 1,000, from London–Brighton to Land's End–John o' Groats, at times even nudging the men's records. Five of her records still stand today, some 65 or more years later. Eileen was born in Coventry in 1923 to Percy and Jeannie Shaw, an engineer and a milliner respectively. Her father was a keen athlete who enjoyed cycling, while her grandfather had been a bike builder who had also raced in the 1890s. Sheridan had a happy, loving childhood, growing up with a quiet, studious older brother who eventually became an engineer. Eileen, on the other hand, was a creative spirit, who fizzed with surplus energy and dreamed of going to art school. Since that wasn't really an option for a working class family from Coventry in the 1940s, she became a secretary in a car show room instead.

She learnt to ride on a heavy old bike which her aunt lent her, but her father soon bought her a lighter frame on which she would go off exploring the countryside around Coventry. She met other teenage cyclists, including a boy with a tandem, who perhaps had ambitions beyond friendship. As their rides together got longer and longer, she discovered she was much stronger in the final miles, ensuring they got home at a good snappy pace which avoided any unnecessary lingering.

At home by the Thames, Eileen writes her autobiography, Wonder Wheels, published in 1956.
© Eileen Sheridan

Sheridan was a teenager when the war broke out. Her family survived the Blitz, even though their house got hit by an incendiary bomb. One day she was at the local outdoor pool when she spotted a 'dark eyed black haired young man who swam like an otter', as she later wrote in her autobiography. Ken Sheridan was an engineer from London, working in one of the local factories as part of the war effort. He was also a keen athlete who loved cycling, and they lost no time falling in love. At weekends the two of them would escape the bombed-out city and go for long rides in the countryside. Perhaps knowing the random tragedies of war could end their happiness at any moment only intensified their pleasure in each other's company. A year after first meeting they were married.

They joined the Cyclists Touring Club (CTC), and would go on long group rides. On one occasion, Eileen was the only girl in a group doing a 140-mile run in 12 hours. The more experienced riders presumably had their doubts about her ability to keep up and kept checking solicitously on her wellbeing – maybe they had train stations in the backs of their minds where they might drop her off. By the end of the ride, however, it was Eileen, fresh and buoyant as ever, having to rally her significantly more tired companions.

In 1944 Ken bought her a lightweight racing bike, and they joined the Coventry Cycle Club, where they thought they might have a go at racing. Eileen entered the club's 10-mile time trial and not only won it, but set a new club record. That was her first race. When she rode her first full season the following year, she ended up winning the national championship 25-mile time trial.

Their son Clive was born the following year, and within seven weeks of his birth Eileen was training again. Ken set up a trailer for the baby so they could continue riding together, and she was soon back to her old ways, now winning time trials in 50- and 100-mile distances.

In 1949 she thought she might have a go at the Yorkshire Cycling Federation's 12-hour race. It was a big leap from 100s she'd done, which the best women at the time were riding in a little under five hours. Ken wasn't keen; a '12' was not something to be undertaken lightly and besides, they had a lot of bills to pay and could ill afford additional costs. Their club mates, however, were keen to see what their pocket-sized champion could achieve, and offered to get Eileen to the race and provide backup. So she set sail, and only went and smashed the record, covering 237.62 miles, beating a record Suzy Rimmington had set the previous year by some 17 miles. The victory must have been all the sweeter since in 1948 Rimmington had beaten Sheridan by the smallest of margins to get the inaugural BAR (Best All Rounder), an award given at the end of the year to the rider with the fastest average times over three set distances. Sheridan would have ridden even further, had she not backtracked at one point, worried that she'd gone off course. By the end of the season it was Eileen's turn to win the BAR. She also became the second woman after Marguerite Wilson to win the highly prestigious Bidlake memorial prize.

By 1950 she was indubitably the star of British women's cycling. Looking for new challenges, she was receptive to the idea of tackling some place-to-place records, which Mary Rawlinson, the secretary of the WRRA (Women's Road Records Association) suggested she try. Eileen duly despatched the records for Birmingham–London and London–Oxford–London.

In 1951 Raleigh got in touch with her and asked her if she would like to try for some records under their name. They were offering £500 if she managed the lot. It wasn't a great deal of money, and it's important to point out that Eileen would have lost her amateur status, which meant, in turn, her right to compete in time

trials, which she loved. As far as the National Cyclists Union was concerned, accepting sponsorship was like losing your virginity: once you'd been 'tainted' by professionalism, there was no going back to the amateur ranks. Ken thought the Raleigh offer was a bit rubbish and encouraged Eileen to turn it down. Not long after that, Hercules came knocking with a much better proposal: a salary and a bonus of £1 a mile for every record she took. (This would have been about £24 in today's money. The combined distance of all the records was more than 3,000 miles, so she would potentially have received more than £72,000 in today's money).

Sheridan was not only well paid, but she also had a coach, Frank Southall who had guided Marguerite Wilson through her record-breaking attempts just before the war.

That said, he didn't seem to do much coaching. Eileen had no idea which records she would be breaking or when – it all depended on the weather and the availability of officials. At home Ken set up a gym in the garage, where he helped her work on strength. The rest of the time she simply rode long distances, as fast as she could. Sometimes she would ride as much as 400—500 miles a week. That seemed to work for Eileen. She applied herself to each attempt with gusto, and the records tumbled. She made it seem easy.

She improved the 100-mile record by 15 minutes and broke the women's hour record at the Herne Hill velodrome with a distance of 23 miles 975 yards. On her Liverpool to Edinburgh ride she even beat a time Southall himself had set in 1935. One of the rules that went with the record-breaking attempts, established in 1890, was that there could be no advance publicity, so they were done in secrecy and there were no roadside fans who could support and cheer Eileen in her efforts. There would be volunteers from local clubs managing checkpoints or helping wave her through red lights in towns, but she barely saw them. It must have been a bit lonely at times.

It must have also been quite hard to keep up the pace with all those many miles spooling out ahead. In an interview with Jack Thurston, Eileen talked about the kick she got from playing cat and mouse with other riders, 'No one ever passed me in time trials, I used to chase and catch. It was a great thrill, it really was.' But in these record attempts there was no one to set her sights on up the road. Just a man with a stopwatch in the car behind. In October 1952 came her first really big challenge, and her 13th record of the year, the 287 miles from Land's End to London. Despite the hilly route and adverse weather, she rode strongly with a time of 16:45:47, breaking Wilson's record by 23 minutes and 13 seconds. Coming into London there were crowds of spectators cheering her on. Given that no one was supposed to know this made her uneasy, to say the least, and her suspicions were confirmed on arrival: somehow the press had got wind of the attempt and written about it, which meant her record would not be recognised. Eileen was aghast, as you well would be, if you'd spent nearly 17 hours riding as fast as you could against the wind, the hills and the jolting road, all the while trying not to nod off and crash into a ditch.

But worse was to come; Frank Southall wanted her to continue riding, to make it an (unofficial) 24-hour record. Eileen was dismayed, as was the crowd which had gathered around them, supporting her with shouts of 'don't you do it love!' The WRRA later spent 2½ hours deliberating whether to let the record pass, but decided to stick to the rules. They had a reputation for integrity which they had to uphold at all costs and it was a founding principal never to give the men cause to criticise their actions.

Later, however, Eileen was told that if Hercules had launched an appeal, the WRRA would probably have relented. Hercules, however, had no interest in doing so since the scandal brought them excellent press coverage. Which inevitably makes one suspicious as to how the information got leaked in the first place. Sheridan swiftly moved on, and a year later did the same ride again, this time improving her unofficial record by more than two hours. In Ireland, where the 1890 rule didn't apply, she rode from Galway–Dublin, and from Cork–Dublin to wildly enthusiastic crowds. Whether it was thanks to their encouragement or her superlative from, Sheridan easily broke the women's records, as well as the men's, into the bargain.

In 1954 her record breaking culminated with her most heroic ride, the 870 miles from Land's End to John o' Groats. Some pretty impressive riders had already set records on this distance. The first had been Lilian Dredge, in 1938, followed by Marguerite Wilson in 1939 with a time of 2 days, 22 hours and 52 minutes. In 1953 another pint-sized champion from Coventry, Edith Atkins, had set a new record of 2 days, 18 hours and four minutes. Unlike Wilson, who was sponsored and had a team of paid helpers, Atkins only had her husband to help. The ride strikes fear into the heart of any cyclist not simply because of its length, but the difficulty of the terrain – there are so many hills, many of them steep – and the fact that the weather is invariably bad. Eileen did a reconnaissance of the route by car with Southall, and was daunted. Worse, there was talk of carrying on beyond John o' Groats to set a new 1,000-mile record while she was at it. At 10am on 6 July she set off on her greatest challenge yet, smiling cheerfully as usual, and rode 470 miles to Carlisle without stopping, other than to put on rain gear. She was in pretty good spirits, though two hours behind an ambitious schedule which Southall had set for her. She battled fierce winds across the Scottish borders, yet slowly caught up on her target times and then started to pull ahead. She continued to ride through the night across the Grampians

> She applied herself to each attempt with gusto, and the records tumbled. She made it seem easy.

between Perth and Inverness. By dawn, the 'Mighty Atom', as the press nicknamed her, was cold and exhausted, having ridden through two nights without sleeping. She wasn't wearing gloves, and her hands became so blistered that she could barely hold onto her handlebars. She rested for an hour, then plugged on, through a constant barrage of hills. With only three gears, she was sometimes obliged to get off and walk up some of the stiff gradients. As she drew closer to John o' Groats she rode into a headwind and a sea mist that chilled her to the bone. She piled on extra layers, including one of Southall's sweaters, but nothing seemed to help.

And then she was there – crossing a final bluff, she saw she only had a few hundred yards left to the hotel, and managed a final sprint to the finish. She had smashed Wilson's record by nearly 12 hours. But the torture was far from over. There was still the little matter of riding a further 130 miles to clinch a 1,000-mile record. So at 11pm, after less than two hours' sleep, she set off again into the dark. It took her 12 hours to ride those last 130 miles (when, in top form that year, she had shown she could ride 250 miles in the same time). She should not have been on the bike. She should have been tucked up in bed with five blankets and a hot water bottle. 'If you could just increase your speed by a third of a mile per hour, love, you could beat the men's record,' Southall had told her. But Eileen was zigzagging across the road and talking to ghosts. After 60 miles she had to stop and sleep. Fried eggs and bacon were prepared and she was fed like a baby, as she slumped in the seat of the caravan, unable to hold a fork let along bring it to her mouth.

A bit of a food and rest can work miracles though. She forged valiantly on over the last 40 miles, even increasing her speed to 20mph at points. Finally, at 11am, she was back at John o' Groats. With her overall time of 3 days and 1 hour, she was 2 hours short of the men's record but had beaten that of the great Hubert Opperman, established in 1934. And that was pretty much that. She took a month off, then knocked out a 50-mile record and signed off with a fine '25'. It was the only record that she couldn't crack straight away, complaining afterwards that it took her 25 miles normally just to get warmed up. Her competitive cycling days were done. Her daughter was born in 1955 and Eileen moved onto other things. Perhaps, with her background in cycle touring for the sheer pleasure of it, she was able to walk away from her brilliant career without any regrets. She and Ken continued to ride, and she rediscovered her artistic bent, taking up glass engraving which would become her life's other great passion.

Eileen features in a Pathé newsreel from 1956 which declares, 'No wonder she wins races. She has to – to get back in time to catch up with the housework.' Eileen probably did have her work cut out for her with the children, but she was also a woman who had it all: a devoted husband, the bike, the accolades, the money, the adventures, the gorgeous children. She won, in every way.

LYLI HERSE

'The Goddess of Randonneurs'

Cycling histories often have a fairy tale quality to them, and Lyli's childhood fits this pattern. Between the age of one and six Lyli was brought up by an aunt in Dieppe, some 170km away from her parents who lived in the Parisian suburb of Levallois-Perret and were struggling to make ends meet. For five years they used packing cases for furniture.

Lyli was finally reunited with her parents when she was six and a half. Things hadn't got much easier. Within a few months, she had to get up and go to school on her own: her parents would leave for work at 5.30am. After school she would come home alone, prepare dinner, and bring it to her father's workshop where she would eat with her parents. 'Then I would go home, wash the dishes and go to bed.'

During school holidays Lyli was sent away again to live – and work – on farms. She was up at dawn to help milk the cows and throughout the day there was never an idle moment. 'But', she said, 'I was almost happy to do this. I loved my parents dearly and I wanted to help them in every way I could.'

Lyli, who was christened Lysiane, was a shy, conscientious, diminutive child. Who could have imagined that this melancholic looking little scrap of a girl would win 200km-long races over mountains like the Galibier and the Tourmalet during a ten-year amateur cycling career? Or that she would dominate the French national road race championships for a further decade, winning eight national titles? Who could imagine that she would later become a tough, no-nonsense coach who would guide Geneviève Gambillon through two world championship victories and 22 national championship titles?

Lyli had one advantage over other children in her situation; her father René would become the finest bicycle maker France has ever produced. A René Herse was the Bentley of the bike world, a bespoke, handcrafted masterpiece of thoughtful engineering, as pleasurable to ride as to behold. They called him the 'couturier' of bikes and the metaphor was quite correct.

René started out as an aeronautical engineer in the Bréguet factory where he was part of the team that built the first plane to fly from Europe to America against the prevailing westerly wind. He brought the rigour and technical innovation of his aviation background to bicycle design and construction, together with a constant quest for strength and lightness. René made almost everything himself, from the chainsets to the stems, racks, mudguards and bells. Even the handlebars were individually shaped, in a process that could take the best part of a day to complete. His attention to detail led him to fashion his own nuts and bolts. Many of his innovations – he was the first to hide cables in the frame – are still in use today. He was one of part of a Parisian cottage industry that now no longer exists, relying on enamellers, chrome platers and wheel builders dotted across the city in small workshops like his own.

Cycling was the centre of the Herse family's life. Every Sunday, come rain or shine, they would be out on their bikes, bringing young Lyli with them. She would say that she was pedalling before she was born, since her mother Marcelle set a new record for Paris–Dieppe just three months before Lyli was born.

As René's reputation grew, he was asked to build frames for many top riders, including Tour de France champions Louison Bobet and Jacques Anquetil and Olympic champion Guy Lapébie. He was popular with Belgian professionals too, with two-time world champion Briek Schotte among the many who beat a path to his door. René would make the bikes, then get them painted and badged with the insignia of the riders' commercial sponsors. René's core market, however, was the thriving amateur scene for whom cycling represented another way of life: weekend escapes from the city, affordable holidays and perhaps the possibility of romance. These riders were part of the Herse family's social circle, and for them he designed touring frames and tandems that were responsive, lightweight and strong.

The amateur cycling scene in France during and after the Second World War was – as it remains – a rather splintered church. Trying to get a handle on the different sects and their acronyms is guaranteed to bring on a headache, but it helps to understand the culture from which Lyli emerged and which ultimately defined her.

We might start with the Audax riders (always with a capital A) who were inspired by a group of Italian friends in the late 1890s, who wanted to see what distance they could cover between sunrise and sunset. (*Audax* is the Latin for *audacious*.) In 1904 Henri Desgrange, who had created the Tour de France in 1903, spoiled the fun by taking ownership of the Italians' idea and giving it rules, the most important of which is that Audax *is never about racing*. Then, as now, Audax riders travel in packs covering great set distances, such as 200, 400 or even 600km, at a strictly enforced average speed (these days around 22.5km/h). Every group has a captain who must on no account be overtaken. Audax offered the common man a means of attaining greatness, without having to win races or break into an ungentlemanly sweat.

In 1921 there was a schism, leading to two clubs, the Audax Club Parisien (ACP) and the Union des Audax Clubs Parisiens (can you spot the difference?) which eventually changed its name to the (much less confusing) Union des Audax Français (UAF). The ACP were the rebels, whose riders were now allowed to ride a bit faster if they fancied and might even choose their companions according to whim, without forgetting that *it's still not a race, even if you finish first*. Both sects have separate governing bodies even now. Then there were *cyclotouristes*, the Herse's tribe, who might go camping together, but who also liked to test themselves with races that were the precursors of modern *cyclosportives*. Unlike today's cyclosportive participants, however, Lyli's contemporaries took pains to always look like they were on holiday. Race rules even stipulated they rode with mudguards and racks and carried a minimum weight in their panniers. Instead of the close-fitting woollen shorts and jerseys favoured by the pros, *cyclotouristes* would wear tailored flannel shorts with their shirts neatly tucked under their belts.

Teenage Lyli, à bloc. Randonnée de Cyclotourisme au Moulin de Sannois. © Presse Sports/Offside

Despite these handicaps, there were some very competitive riders whose dedication to racing hard could be compared to the top time trial and place-to-place riders in Britain of the same period. Just as in the UK, the amateur racing scene was also significant for women who, in the absence of officially sanctioned road races, could use these events to express their athletic prowess.

All these amateur sects – who, at the risk of offending purists, we might group together under the church of *randonneurs* – had, despite their differences, far more in common with each other than the professionals, or *coureurs*. Where *coureurs* try to win at all costs, *randonneurs* help fix each other's punctures and they don't abandon the weak. They are the tortoises to racing's hares, champions of long distance endurance, persistence, saddlebags and reflector belts.

Having just said all that, in the early 20th century, professional and amateur cycling sometimes overlapped in a way that seems inconceivable now. The Tour de France, in its earliest days, had one category for the 'aces' and another for amateurs, who could ride the whole route or just take part in one stage.

The *Polymultipliée de Chanteloup*, first held in 1913, was another race for both amateurs and professionals (its founder was a member of the ACP). Held on a hilly course west of Paris, with the intention of showcasing the benefits of a derailleur, the professional race for men featured multiple laps of a roughly 10k circuit with a number of hard climbs, including one with a 14% gradient. Any rider found dismounting was immediately disqualified. (The race eventually became the *Trophée des Grimpeurs*, which ran until 2009).

When Lyli was growing up, there was also a *Polymultipliée* mixed tandem event for amateurs. Lyli rode her first *Polymultipliée* at the age of 14 and came second. Three years later, in partnership with Robert Prestat, a newspaper delivery man, she won the race in imperious style, smashing the record by seven minutes, riding at an average speed of 33.48km/h (the professional men that year rode at 33.35km/h, albeit on a longer course). Over the next eight years Lyli and Robert would dominate the event, while her father consistently won a technical prize for the best frame builder.

One year the duo crashed and Lyli broke her collarbone. They forged on regardless, even though she had great difficulty pulling on the handlebars on climbs. 'And then the bone came out and ended up sticking out of my jersey,' Lyli recalled. Astonishingly, they not only finished the race, but won it, yet again. Unfortunately the crash also broke a mudguard, as a result of which they failed the post-race technical check-up and were disqualified (René subsequently improved his design).

After the race, Lyli remembered a soigneur and his colleague trying to put her collarbone back in place. 'They spent about 10 minutes trying to manipulate it but they had to give up in the end. He told me, "we'll have to take you to hospital so you can get it operated on. They'll need to put a plate in there to keep it in place."' At that point Lyli burst into tears. 'The thought of being put to sleep in a hospital absolutely terrified me. The soigneur couldn't believe it. He said, we've just spent ten minutes trying to put your collarbone back in place and you haven't made a sound, and you only start crying now, when we talk about hospital!'

Lyli and Robert became the fastest mixed tandem crew in France and were frequently stronger than male teams. In 1949 they won the overall tandem category of the amateur edition of the *Boucles de la Seine*, a 270km race sponsored by the Communist newspapers *Ce Soir* and *l'Humanité*, which skirted around the loops of the river Seine as it meanders across Paris and the Ile de France. The tandem racers must have been quite a sight, thrashing round courses at terrific speed, or scrambling through forests on cyclocross races, the captain and stoker carefully co-ordinated, not just in their efforts but in their attire. While professional jerseys were prohibited, riders made themselves distinctive in matching tops; check shirts, Breton stripes, or more traditional cycling jerseys with graphic colour blocking. Lyli made quite a few of these herself, bringing her knitting needles to settle nerves before races.

One of her specials featured a looping fleur-de-lys motif in the colours of her club which she wore with another tandem partner, Yves 'Chou Chou' Cohen, who would later join the pro ranks and race with Coppi and Anquetil.

When I first met Lyli in 2017, she was living in a small, white bungalow, built by her parents in the early 70s, in a cul-de-sac on the edge of a forest in the Vexin, just beyond the tentacle tips of the suburban RER trains that serve Paris. If you cycled from the station, you'd work up a good sweat riding the two or three kilometres of one of those climbs that never seem to let up: you think you're about to reach the crest and then you turn a corner and the road just keeps on rising through the trees. Lyli lived at the summit of one of these climbs, on the route of the *Polymultipliée*. She had been widowed for a few years, and lived on her own with her rescue dog.

She was tiny and neat as a pin, with cropped white hair and pale, inquisitive eyes, astonishingly vital for her 89 years. She would tell her stories with a wry little smile and a tip of the head to emphasise a point. She showed me her exercise bike in a small room covered in dark wallpaper with a gigantic floral motif. On the walls were photos of her parents, her late husband and her most cherished race victories. She had a calendar on which she wrote down her mileage; by November 2017 she'd ridden 7,500km for the year.

She was delighted I'd ridden up her hill on my bike. 'Climbing was my cup of tea', she said, explaining that she had exceptionally long femurs, which gave her a special advantage in terms of leverage. She said races like the *Polymultipliée* set her up for later in her career. 'I won races that I shouldn't have because the other girls didn't know how to use a derailleur. They would race first into the hairpins, but I'd sit behind them and then go past them using the big chain ring coming out of the bends. That was a technique I learnt as a *cyclotouriste*.' She said you could give her a steep hill over a false flat any day.

She broke records in the *Brevet Randonneur des Alpes,* a 245km loop starting in Grenoble which featured the col du Glandon, the col de la Croix de Fer, the col du Télégraphe and the col du Galibier mountain passes, which she rode in 11h47m, and in the *Randonnée des Cols Pyréneens*, or RCP, whose 192km from Pau to Luchon (and vice versa on alternate years) went over the col d'Aubisque, the col du Tourmalet, the col d'Aspin, and the col de Peyresourde. She did this in 9h30m.

In 1951 Lyli set a record even Jeannie Longo has failed to break, riding up the Puy-de-Dôme, the plug of a long extinct volcano overlooking Clermont-Ferrand in the Massif Central. It takes 15km of slowly spiralling road, mostly at a gradient of 9%, to reach the top. The last 5km are at 12%. It is the setting for one of the most famous photographs in Tour de France history, of Jacques Anquetil and

Raymond Poulidor, shoulder to shoulder, in a desperate duel that will decide the outcome of the entire race. Riding through great gusts of wind, Lyli managed the climb in 55 minutes, prompting the writer Henri de la Tombelle to compare her to David tackling Goliath. He called her the 'goddess' of all *randonneurs*, but also commented on, 'her modesty, her rather sad face, somewhat drowned in indifference, which contrasts so much with the "winner's laugh".' Lyli never hung around when she won, preferring to melt away into the crowd. 'I wasn't especially proud of my victories', she said. 'Everything I did was for my parents.'

Amongst his many customers René Herse counted Jean Leulliot, a well-known journalist and race-organiser, who ran *Paris–Nice*. He was famous for his crazy, inventive ideas that earned him the nickname '*Unidéparjour*' (an-idea-a-day). One year *Paris–Nice* became *Paris–Nice–Rome*. He created a *Tour d'Europe*. Less gloriously, he collaborated with the Nazis to create an ersatz Tour de France during the War.

In 1955 Leulliot said Lyli should get herself a proper racing licence. He was launching a women's Tour de France, and perhaps he had her in mind as its star. She certainly lived up to expectations, winning both the first and last stages and coming fourth overall. She held the leader's jersey for most of the race until a British racing cyclist, Millie Robinson, won the fourth day's stage and consolidated her position with a dominating time trial on the fifth and final day. Leulliot was not impressed, however. 'Afterwards he told me, you'll never make a good rider, you're too nice', she said. 'He was right,' she added 'I had grown up in the spirit of cyclotourism. If I knew someone was behind trying to overtake me in a race, I'd 'open the door' and let her get past, even if I might try to chase her down later.'

She remained a cyclotouriste at heart, even while winning races. At a national championship one year in Sancerre: 'I broke away, then punctured, with three laps to go. The girls passed me but I caught back up with them. I attacked again and this time rode into a terrible wind, although I tried to shelter behind hedges. But I still looked left and right. At one point there was the most beautiful view, with sheep and clouds and dramatic light. Afterwards I told my father, "if I'd had a camera I would have stopped to take a picture."'

She won races by tiring out her rivals and then launching attacks, and complained that the elite women's races were never long enough: the national championships were mostly less than 70km. She won her first national championship in 1956. The prize was an old miner's lamp which had its previous owner's number stamped onto it. When she finally married, much later in life, her husband turned it into an electric light, which sat on a shelf in her sitting room.

Lyli got her revenge on the British by winning the points jersey, the mountains jersey and the overall of the eight stage Circuit Lyonnais Forest–Auvergne in 1958. A British rider, Mayers, came third. Lyli retired after winning her eighth and final national championship in 1967, at the age of 39. Her father, who coached her and came to her races, was starting to suffer from health problems. 'There was never any money in racing,' she said. Her reward was the publicity it brought her parents' business and the bouquet she brought back for her mother.

Lyli said her greatest regret was that her father never taught her how to weld. From the age of 17, she worked 12 hours a day, six days a week in her father's shop. She would run errands, like cycling 10km across town to the enamellers, carrying two frames on her back, 'like a musette'. She learnt to build wheels and assemble bikes. If she could have built the frames themselves, she could have kept the business going when ill health forced both her father and later her husband to retire. Working in the shop, Lyli would meet the famous racing cyclists when they came to pick up their bikes. Did they know that the pretty girl taping up their handlebars was the daughter of the *maitre*, and the French national champion, to boot? Did they talk to her, I wondered? 'Why would they have had any interest in me?' she said with a shrug.

She was a different woman when she coached the VC Levallois-Perret women's team between 1968 and 1975. Danielle Crueize (née Piton) told me they would meet outside the shop at 5am to train and riders and their machines had to be immaculate, or they were sent back home. 'I remember Geneviève Aude's mum saying to me, "well, I know it's all got to be nice and clean, but when Geneviève gets back home she always puts her bike in the bath!"'

'Lyli didn't consider the number of hours you worked,' which in Danielle's case were daunting: a domestic maid, she worked from 7.30am until 9pm, six days a week. If you wanted to win races, whether you felt tired didn't come into it. 'If you sat up a bit too soon for her tastes she'd say, I'm on my bike too. If I'm doing it, so can you. She really understood the science of racing and was very good at reading races. She had her tricks. She taught us how to shelter ourselves. She taught us to relay from in front – in other words when you pulled away for the next rider to come through, you'd accelerate. That way you intimidate her and discourage others from attacking.'

'Lyli was very tough,' says Danielle. 'You had the impression she had no emotions. It's only later that I understood that she loved her parents dearly. They were very important for her. It's a shame, because she didn't live her own life. She was slender and charming. She threw herself into her parent's business and forgot about herself.'

Lyli's father died the day after he moved into the house he'd had built. Her mother died two years later. At the age of 48 Lyli was left alone in the world. 'I still miss them tremendously,' she told me. Two years later she married Jean Desbois, her father's right hand man who bore an uncanny resemblance to René. 'My father never had a bad word to say about him,' said Lyli. 'He was like a son to him.' Lyli and Jean kept the business going, but by the 1980s people no longer invested in bikes in the same way they saved up for cars. The Desbois retired, and shut up shop. Jean spent two years working out of their garage fulfilling the remaining orders.

> 'I learnt a lesson I've never forgotten, that you don't get something for nothing.'

I met Lyli again shortly before Christmas when she invited me round for lunch. We had creamed spinach, a hard-boiled egg and a rasher of crispy bacon, and we talked about food. She told me about the farm she'd stayed on as a child and how she screwed up all her courage one day to ask the farmer's wife whether she might eat one of the ears of a pig that was about to be slaughtered. Certainly, said the *matrone*, you can have the ear: but first you peel the 5 kilos of onions we'll need for the black pudding. 'I think I cried every tear in my body,' Lyli said, who worked her way through the eye-watering onions, but she got her prize. 'I learnt a lesson I've never forgotten, that you don't get something for nothing.'

She talked about picking nettles with her bare hands for making nettle soup, and how blueberries are good for your eyesight. She told me about how her father sponsored a team which took part in Paris–Brest–Paris and how she'd helped out, providing food for the riders. She gave them celery sticks to chew on at night, 'it helps keep you awake', and she also gave them rice dumplings that had been cooked in sweetened condensed milk and stuffed with an apricot soaked in kirsch.

She invited me to come back in the spring with my daughters. I thought about how pleased they would be about making it up that hill on their bikes, and what an impression this former champion would make on them, with her mining lamp trophy and her needlepoint tapestries and her special tin of biscuits that only came out for guests. 'Don't wait too long,' she'd said. 'I don't intend to stick around forever.'

Lyli died in January 2018, two days short of her 90th birthday. About 25 people attended her funeral, where a pale blue René Herse was propped against a wall and we listened to *La Bicyclette*, an Yves Montand chanson from the 1960s. It's about a group of friends who spend a glorious summer's day on their bikes: four boys and the postman's daughter, Paulette, with whom they're all secretly in love. I can imagine all those randonneurs being a little bit in love with Lyli. Perhaps some of them were there, amongst the elderly gentlemen wiping their eyes.

MILLIE ROBINSON

'The Manx Pixie'

Millie Robinson was the first British rider to win the Tour de France, 57 years before Sir Bradley Wiggins.

Actually, it was more like a five-stage Tour of Normandy, but the race organiser, Jean Leulliot, was a journalist who published his own cycling magazine, *Route et Piste*, and he knew that billing his race as a *Tour de France Féminine* would sell more copies than a *Tour de Normandie*. Afterwards he praised the girls' courage, endurance and enthusiasm. But he had a few complaints, too: he criticised their positioning on their bikes, grumbled that there wasn't enough attacking and felt there was a bit too much chatting. Worst of all, they spent too much time at the end of each stage going shopping.

But in the history of women's racing, it was nonetheless a momentous event. It was only the second stage race for women ever to be held. The first was a three-day event called the Circuit Lyonnais-Auvergne, which had taken place a few months earlier, in July 1955. Millie had won that too. In fact, women's road racing under the official auspices of national federations was still in its infancy. The National Cycling Union in Britain only staged its first 'official' women's national road race championship in 1955 (although the rebel British League of Racing cyclists had already been organising women's championships in 1947).

In France it was a similar story with the socialist sports organisation, the FSGT, organising women's national championships from 1948, and the FFC – the French Cycling Federation – getting in on the act in 1951, so that in France, too, for a period, there were two national championships. In East Germany and Russia there were national championships in the 1950s, but Belgium and Luxembourg dragged their heels until 1959. The Italians didn't commit until 1963. American women had to wait until 1966, West Germans until 1968. Sweden and Norway didn't join the game until 1972 and 1974.

So when Millie and her teammates set out in July for the first French stage race, in Roanne on the North Eastern edge of the Auvergne, it was a bit of an adventure into the unknown. They came back not only with Millie having won each of the three, 70km stages and the overall, but with her teammates June Thackray, Bobby Tingey and Beryl French coming 2nd, 7th and 9th respectively. It was quite a statement.

When they returned for the Tour de France at the end of September, there was a bit of trepidation – as far as the French were concerned – about what they might do next. The English cycling journalist Jock Wadley came to report on the race, and ended up doing a 17-page cover story for the inaugural issue of a new magazine he was publishing, *Coureur*. 'What a rider is Robinson', one French girl said to Wadley before the race. 'She climbs hills without changing gear.'

The British team very nearly missed the race. The signing in ceremony took place in the fancy surroundings of the Printemps department store in the centre of

Paris, where guests of honour included Jean Robic, notorious for winning the first post-war Tour de France by ignoring etiquette and attacking on the final stage, and Louis Gérardin, a recently retired track champion whose 23-year career saw him winning the French national sprint championships 13 times.

Printemps was about to close when the English team finally arrived, hot footing it from their train which had just arrived at the Gare Saint Lazare. They consisted of six riders: Daisy Franks, Joy Bell, Sylvia Whybrow, Beryl French, June Thackray and Millie Robinson. Their manager was Eileen Gray, founder of the Women's Track Racing Association, who had just that year managed to persuade the UCI to ratify women's world record attempts. The support team would be rounded out by Tom Crowther, a frame builder from Derbyshire (and founder of Mercian Cycles) who would act as the team's mechanic, and two chaps from the Altrincham Raven CC, Ken Redford and Nobby Roberts. The majority of women racing were French, holding licences from both the FSGT and FFC federations. There was also one Swiss rider, Marie Louise Vonaburg, and Elsy Jacobs, from Luxembourg. The French looked to provide some robust opposition following their crushing defeat in July. Among their number were Lydia Haritonides, a Parisian rider who had recently beaten Daisy Franks' world 500m record. There was also Lyli Herse, a French rider with an excellent palmarès in France as a cyclo-sportive rider, winning 200km long races-that-weren't-officially-races in the Alps and Pyrenees.

Wadley noted that while 'the promotion of this ambitious race was a triumph for the French racing girls and their considerable number of male supporters', there was also quite a strong public feeling against it, 'largely promoted by a small section of the press.' The following morning the riders assembled at 7am at the Café des Sports, a famous meeting place for riders near the Bois de Boulogne and its famous cyclists' training loop, located at the Porte Maillot end of the Avenue de la Grande Armée, where all the major French cycling brands had their flagship stores.

The Athletic Club Boulogne Billancourt, one of the top Parisian amateur clubs and a stepping-stone for many professional male riders, provided a bus to transport the bikes to the race start in Rambouillet. 'Loudspeakers blared; car engines spluttered in the cold morning air; officials began a minor panic; people called each other unkind names; police blew whistles. It was getting late. The girls embussed. Followers piled into various cars and off we went to Rambouillet.' With 45 minutes to go before the official start, the British team ordered omelettes in a nearby café, 'much to the amazement of some officials and journalists who know that all good bike riders never eat within two hours of a race.'

Wadley got a lift on the Vespa of René de Latour, a French-American correspondent for the *Parisien Libéré*. They decided to bypass the race so

Millie with Lyli, before taking the lead at the 1955 women's Tour de France. © Presse Sports/Offside

they could follow the riders from in front, and as they got back onto the route encountered some professional male riders – Gerardin, Senfftleben, Godeau and Macé – out on a training ride, keen to see the girls. Others waited to cheer them on one of the climbs.

The peloton kept a steady pace of about 23 mph and dropped quite a few riders off the back, but no one was attacking off the front. Neither, when the peloton entered a plain with a crosswind, did riders form echelons, a classic tactic for distancing rivals. Instead, they rode on the right hand side of the road, 'in something resembling a disorderly club run'. It clearly wasn't the real Tour de France. There were other points of difference too: the riders were all amateurs and since quite a few were riding as individuals, there was to be no collaboration or drafting between team members. The first stage ended in a sprint won by Lyli Herse, who took the white jersey of the race leader.

By the third stage Wadley was gently expressing his disappointment that each stage seemed to follow the same rhythm, with the weaker riders falling off the back, the stronger riders always ending in a bunch sprint at the front and no fireworks in between, but this was mainly because the British team were setting such a high pace: 'nobody was really capable of producing the extra dash necessary to open up a gap, or to sustain it if they did.' Millie Robinson, 'being so much in the time trial habit,' was the main culprit up front. 'Had Millie stopped in the middle of the bunch for most of the day and reserved her effort for the end she might have been capable of a solo break over the last miles. But the greater part of Millie's cycling life has been spent bashing away at the front of mostly male club runs or in solitary rides against the watch, and the prospect of taking back wheels in the middle of a bunch has no attractions for her.'

By the end of the third stage in Vimoutiers the British riders were still, 'fresh as paint, waiting for the baggage van with no more fuss than if they had just been for a gentle club run.' This was not the experience of some of the other riders, however. The final part of the race featured three laps over a 2.5km circuit featuring a steep hill. Wadley, 'watched the pitiful spectacle of the various girls dropped off during the race climbing wearily to the line, only to learn they had another two laps to go. Some of them tackled it in tears.' The last rider, 'after completing one lap, fell off her bike, unable to go further. Yet her name appeared on the day's bulletin as completing the 70km, 26 minutes after the leaders, and I'm sure there were no protests that she hadn't.'

The fourth stage provided more excitement, with some steep climbing into Rouen and a tricky section through the city where riders had to negotiate cobbles and tram tracks. A bunch of seven finally broke away, featuring race leader Lyli Herse and her compatriot Marie-Jeanne Donabedian, in 2nd place on GC, and three English riders: Millie, June Thackray and Joy Bell. In Gournay, where the stage finished, Millie broke away and won the stage, getting the leaders' white jersey too, with a lead of only 3 seconds on Lyli, while June came second. The last day featured two stages, with a time trial in the morning before the final race into Mantes-la-Jolie, located on the Seine west of Paris, in the afternoon. Francis Pélissier, the great French champion of the pre-war years, who used to dominate the Bordeaux–Paris race and who had discovered up and coming talent, Jacques Anquetil, turned up before the time trial. The final stage would finish outside his café in Mantes, but he had made his way to Gourlay so that he could offer his support to Donabedian. Donabedian was riding a bike made by La Perle, for whom Pélissier had spent the last decade working as a Directeur Sportif.

Pélissier was as crafty they came – it was not for nothing that he was nicknamed The Sorcerer – and as soon as it was known he was supporting Donabedian, the race organisers scrambled to find a commissaire to sit in his car. 'Francis wouldn't dream of getting nearer to her than 20 metres [the stipulated distance behind which accompanying cars had to follow riders], but he might quite innocently create a small traffic block behind him, then release it suddenly to create momentary pace!' Wadley explained.

'A ride that would, I swear, have beaten half the men time triallists of England.'

For his part, Wadley was to provide backup for Joy, following her in a dairy van, accompanied by 'three men and half a dozen small boys'. Joy was fourth fastest at the end of her ride, and went off to get a coffee while Wadley waited for the other riders to come in. Haritonides crossed the line, but almost immediately afterwards, 'a big girl in blue came tearing for the finish. It was June, one of the new generation of English girls who have specialised in mass start racing, and who now was sprinting to finish a really tremendous time trial', which had not only put her in first position, but also made her virtual race leader. Sylvia Whybrow, Donabedian and Lyli Herse followed and then everyone waited for Millie, the last to start.

'We didn't have to wait for more than a few seconds. Up the road came the maillot blanc from the Isle of Man – and Millie on a man's bike and punching a man's gear and finishing a ride that would, I swear, have beaten half the men time triallists of England', Wadley reported delightedly. The race announcer worked out her average speed – 38.363km/h – and pronounced it 'formidable'.

After a snack of cold rice pudding and tea it was time for the final 49km stage to Mantes, which Wadley considered, 'one of the longest races I have ever followed. Millie had a 35 seconds lead on June, who in turn had 36 seconds in hand over Donabedian. A puncture now to either of them, or a fall – and all their wonderful five days' effort would be wasted.' Indeed this was the fate of French rider Renée Vissac, who had been in 4th place on the GC but lost six minutes due to a puncture. The peloton split into two bunches, with all the British riders in the first, and finished with a sprint outside Pélissier's café, which Lyli Herse won again.

Over dinner that evening there was much talk about the following year's race. Leulliot had already been thinking ahead and had a number of ideas. He wanted to restrict the size of gears, which he already did in the Route de France, a men's amateur stage race. There were plans to make it an official team race, and to invite the Russians. The English girls, for their part, felt the stages 'were neither long enough nor hard enough.'

In the end, Leulliot never organised another women's tour. No matter how modest it might seem in retrospect, it had been a daring initiative, in the face of much negative feeling regarding women racing. Quite a few French journalists considered it a 'stunt race' accordingly to Wadley, while a more supportive reporter was mortified – and received considerable flack from the riders – when his editors rewrote his story, blowing up a humorous aside to make a mockery of the race. It took quite a few more years of campaigning, primarily on Eileen Gray's part, to get the UCI to agree to a women's world championships. When the UCI member countries failed to vote for it in 1957, *L'Equipe* wrote: 'Good sense has triumphed', adding that women 'should be content with existing races and with cyclotourism, which corresponds much better to their muscular abilities.'

But for Wadley, the race had been, on the whole, a great success. 'I got a tremendous kick out of this Tour Féminin, the girls were business-like on their bikes, and ladies off them, their behaviour exemplary.'

For a brief period between 1955 and 1958, Millie became the star of women's cycling. She won the National Cyclists' Union's first ever women's national championship road race in 1955 and again in 1956. She also won the first international women's road race in Britain, held in Harrogate in 1956. Details of races on the Continent are hard to come by but a photo in Yvonne Reynders' biography suggests she also won an international women's race in Putte-Mechelen in Belgium in 1959.

Millie's real forte was in efforts against the clock. Between 1950 and 1959 she took part in 110 time trials, finishing in the top 3 of 104 of them. Her most significant victories were in the British 25-mile championships, which she won three years in a row from 1955 to 1957. She set new British records in the 25, 50 and 100 mile distances, took the hour record in September 1958 and at the end of that season won the very prestigious BAR, or Best all Rounder competition, despite a season-long battle with Beryl Burton, a rising star who desperately wanted it too.
The following year she was eclipsed by Beryl, who would dominate women's cycling in Britain for the next 25 years. That season also marked the end of

Millie's racing career, though remarkably she bore no bitterness towards her rival. The two women were good friends off the bike, Beryl later remembering her as 'a happy character, always ready with a joke, but on the bike she turned to grim determination.'

For all her importance in the history of women's road racing, Millie is largely forgotten now. It took several months to find out what had become of her, let alone whether she was still alive. When I eventually made contact with relatives, they shared many treasures from her scrapbooks with me, including typed up notes and speeches for cycling club dinners that reveal a modest, sweet-natured character with a slapstick sense of humour.

In one document she recalls that the first bike she rode in the Irish farmyard where she grew up, was 'one that never had any punctures since it didn't have any tyres'. In her first race as a club rider, 'they forgot to tell me it was only once round the track, and I went round a couple of times before I heard everyone shouting that I had finished.' She rode her first time trial 'with my mudguards and lamps on, as then I didn't realise you had to strip down, the bike I mean of course.'

Born Mildred Jessie Robinson in County Mayo in 1924, she grew up in a family of nine children, and had an older brother who would later race in Ireland. Her family moved to Peel on the Isle of Man when she was 10, where she would spend most of her life. She served in the Manx Women's Land Army during the War where she earned a reputation for hard work, and began cycling in earnest after joining the Manx Viking Wheelers when she started working in Douglas.

She rapidly became one of the top riders on the island – although you are left to read this between the lines from her notes – and started getting the ferry over to England at weekends to take part in time trials around Liverpool and Manchester. Finally she moved to England in 1955 in order to better realise her ambitions, 'which were mainly the national 25 championship, the British Best All Rounder and the World Hour Record.'

> **For all her importance in the history of women's road racing, Millie is largely forgotten now.**

She had a brother who ran a haulage company in Leeds, and she began working as a truck driver. Later she would get a job at the Raleigh factory, building wheels and testing new frames. Through her links with Raleigh she got to know Reg Harris, the great British track star of the 1940s and 1950s, and it was partly with thanks to his technical advice and connections that she was able to break the hour record in 1958 in Milan.

In late September that year, a few weeks after the inaugural women's world championships, Millie left work on a Friday evening and she and Reg Harris took the plane to Milan. Two months previously, Harris had tested her at his eponymously named velodrome in Manchester. She not only broke the British women's hour record, but also the world record by 9 yards. She hadn't expected to ride so well – the English track, being entirely open to the elements with a concrete surface, was much slower than the partially covered Vigorelli velodrome in Milan with its wooden boards. As a result, there hadn't been any of the controls in place for her world record to be officially ratified.

In Milan she watched French rider Roger Rivière with great admiration as he broke the men's hour the day before her own attempt. His compatriot Renée Vissac was also hanging around the track, hoping to improve on her own record, set the previous year, of 38.569km. She insisted on having another stab at it should Millie beat her, which meant Millie's attempt was scheduled for 4.30pm, when the weather was gusty, instead of Millie's preferred time of 6pm when the wind had normally settled.

Despite the less than ideal conditions, on 25 September 1958 Millie set a new record, with a distance of 39.719km, an improvement of 1,150m on Vissac. At the same time she also broke women's world records at the 10 and 20km. It was one achievement on Millie's palmarès that Beryl Burton was never able to match.

Millie returned to the Isle of Man in 1960, where she became a very talented golfer and yachtswoman and joined a number of antiquarian and natural history societies. At one point she was co-owner of a sign-writing business. At another point she worked as a women's prison warden. She died in 1994, never having married or had children. She is fondly remembered by her two nephews, Roger and Kevin Christian. The latter now safeguards her many scrapbooks, cuttings and trophies. Kevin remembers visiting her in her final days when she was dying of cancer. 'Her parting words were simply, "I wish I had more time."'

ELSY JACOBS

'The Grand Duchess'

Elsy Jacobs has her place in the history of women's cycling for winning the first ever women's world championship road race, in 1958. She turned out to be the perfect champion for all the doubters too, who worried the race would offer distressing scenes of haggard women collapsing in ditches. Not only had she ridden with great panache, but her effervescent joy at winning – in Reims, the champagne capital – her delighted grins as she was hoisted in triumph on her supporters' shoulders, and the fact she was clearly in resplendent health rather than broken and bedraggled, went a long way in assuaging people's fears.

The race was held on a hilly, 20km motor racing circuit featuring one particularly difficult climb called Le Calvaire. Whereas the men's race the following day would feature 14 laps of this circuit, the women only had three, but opponents of women's racing nonetheless thought even that might be too much. 29 riders from 8 different countries took part, and when they hit the climb a small group went away, featuring three Russians, two French riders, one Briton and Elsy, riding for Luxembourg, a country whose cycling federation disapproved of women's racing.

The second time round Elsy broke away, reaching the summit 20 seconds ahead of the rest of the group. Sprinting was not one of her strengths, so she put her head down and forged ahead, keen to sustain a respectable gap on the riders behind. The others no doubt thought she wouldn't be able to sustain the pace and assumed they'd reel her in well before the finish. They were wrong, and by the time they realised their mistake, it was too late. Elsy stormed across the finish line more than two minutes ahead of her pursuers. Then, after savouring her victory, she ran back to cheer the others as they sprinted for second place.

Amid the ovations and euphoria of the crowds of supporters, there were panicked race officials who had forgotten to organise a winner's bouquet. Jacques Grello, a famous singer who also penned a column in the sports magazine *But et Club*, wrote that Elsy's 'communicative warmth ... managed to put us a little bit at ease. She's very good, Elvie. From gritting her teeth in effort she gnawed away her lipstick, but the ringlets of her perm held up well!' Dreadful as those comments sound now, we might cut Grello just a tiny bit of slack given the general obsession with grooming and appearance in the 1950s. Grello also came up with the nick-name *'Pédalleur de Charme'* for Hugo Koblet, who, we shouldn't forget, carried a comb and a sponge in his back pocket so he could spruce up before winning a race. At one point the Tour de France even had a daily prize for the most appealing rider. Anyway, perm or no perm, there was no doubting that Elsy was a star.

She had been ready for this moment since she first fell in love with the sport as a young girl. She was born to farming parents in Garnich in Luxembourg in 1933 and grew up with four older brothers who all raced, one of whom, Edmond, would later ride in the Tour de France. She learnt to ride on her brothers' bikes, and would take off on long rides into the country.

Elsy was effectively the only girl in the family – her older sister Cecile had moved to London – and had to fend for herself within the family pecking order. Small but sassy, she was quite up to the task. She was also hardworking and determined, and didn't flinch at getting stuck into the numerous daily chores, whether that meant helping cook huge meals for her hungry family or helping with the harvest – once she dug up 250kg potatoes in one day. She would plough through her work quickly so that she could spend the afternoon on her bike.

100km sorties soon became routine, and by the time she was 18 she was keen to have a go at racing herself. The Luxembourg cycling federation, however, refused to give her a licence.

Unperturbed, Elsy took part in small, unofficial races in Belgium and France, talking the organisers into letting her participate, even without the right documents. This was not sustainable, however, and by 1953 she had joined a club in Paris, some 330km away, so that she could compete.

The following year the director of the Dippach Cycling Club, a man called Alphonse Risch, wanted two of Elsy's brothers, Raymond and Edmond, on his roster. He also wanted Elsy, and thought that if he offered her a bike, a jersey and travel expenses, that might do the trick in getting the brothers to join too – and it did. The club's trainer, Arny Franck, quickly saw that Elsy had the makings of a great rider, but little tactical nous – she simply rode hard and fast – so he set about teaching her a few tricks of the trade.

In 1957 Elsy finally decided to move to Paris, which by this point was the heartland of women's road racing. She rode for the club CSM Puteaux, initially supporting herself by working as a secretary and child-minder to the club's president.

The 1958 season marked the high point of her long cycling career, when she was 25. She took part in 42 races and won 25 of them, finishing on the podium in all but four. A few months after winning the world championships she travelled to the Vigorelli velodrome in Milan to have a crack at the hour record which Millie Robinson had set only two months previously with a ride of 39.719km. Elsy extended that by more than 1½ km, breaking the 40km barrier with a new record of 41.347km. It wasn't until 1972 that an Italian rider, Maria Cressari, would manage to break the record again. In 1959 Luxembourg finally introduced a women's national championship, of which Elsy won every single edition until 1974, the only exception being in 1969 when she didn't race.

She took part in 15 world championships during her career and while she frequently figured in the top 10, she only managed to get on the podium again in 1961, behind Yvonne Reynders and Beryl Burton. The spectators cheering those three women were witnessing the three greatest riders of a golden age of women's racing. If Burton was the strongest and Reynders the craftiest, then Jacobs was the most exciting rider, an unpredictable firecracker who was always on the attack.

She was so popular with race organisers that she had a regular income from racing, which was quite unheard of in women's cycling at the time. She was a notoriously tough negotiator, good at extracting decent attendance fees. On one occasion she persuaded a promoter to pay top billing for her friend Jeannette Augusto, who she claimed was the Portuguese national champion. Never mind the fact that the Portuguese didn't have national championships for women, or that Augusto, despite her Portuguese roots, was as French as they come.

She also had commercial sponsors, at one point riding in the colours of one of the most powerful men's teams of the time, St Raphaël Géminiani, whose champions included Jacques Anquetil, Rudi Altig and Roger Walkowiak.

If her palmarès was immense, so was her fiery and determined personality. She had an incandescent desire to win and was furious when beaten.

> She had an incandescent desire to win and was furious when beaten.

Yvonne Reynders had been a good friend, and Elsy would often stay with her when she raced in Belgium. Before the 1959 world championships, the two riders were sharing a hotel room and Elsy was tossing and turning unable to sleep. Finally Yvonne heard Elsy's voice out of the dark; 'Whoever wins this race will become my worst enemy.' 'And what if it's me?' asked Yvonne.

'I'll never speak to you again.'

Yvonne went and won the race anyway, 'and from that day she never spoke to me again,' she recalled. 'I think we both suffered for it!' Elsy's hot temper would directly affect her career. In 1974 she was told that she couldn't represent Luxembourg at the world championships in Montreal, regardless of her track record as the indomitable national champion. Her offer to pay her own way was rebuffed. In fury she changed her nationality and became French. While, in some respects, it wasn't such a strange thing to do – she'd lived most of her adult life in France – it effectively ended her international racing career. She might have patched things up with the federation and represented Luxembourg for quite a few more years, but in France the talent pool was much larger. Good as Elsy was, she couldn't make the cut against the ambitious new crop of riders half her age.

Retiring wasn't really Elsy's thing, however. Between 1955 and 1978, when she had to put her racing on hold following an accident, she took part in 1,059 races, of which she won 301, came second in 210 and third in 129. It was while she was convalescing, at the age of 45, that she met the man she would eventually marry. She went to live with him in Britanny, the heartland of French grass roots racing. She raced less, but began mentoring and coaching young riders in her club.

One of these, Valérie Jan, recalled a race in which, 'Elsy was standing in the spot where I was supposed to attack and surprise the others. I attacked and I won my first race on the 1st of May 1983 at home in Loudéac, thanks to Elsy.'

Many other riders would testify to the lessons in race craft Elsy imparted. 'She taught me that you can still go, even when you think you're at your limits', says Danielle Crueize (née Piton), who raced against her in the late 1960s and early 1970s. She remembered one occasion when she'd had to stop to fix her rear wheel. Not long after reconnecting with the bunch she saw Elsy go on the attack. 'I managed to get on the back of her wheel, and then she swung aside so I could go through and do my turn in front. I said, "Oh no, I'm finished", and she said "No you're not". And she was right. So I did my turn and we got away and at the finish I beat her. Afterwards the race speaker said to Elsy, "So, you let Danielle Piton win the race!" And Elsy, who was on the microphone, said, "No, I never let anyone win a race. If Danielle won it, it was because she was the stronger rider."'

Riders remembered her as the life and soul of the party, brimful of energy, an adventurer who got into crazy scrapes, a generous friend who spent her money as quickly as it came in, a food lover who was constantly watching her weight.

The French track cyclist Isabelle Nicoloso recalled being part of a group of riders travelling back from a race with Elsy, who had bought a huge amount of beans at a bargain price just before boarding the train. 'And so that "we shouldn't get too bored" on our journey, she asked us – and all the other passengers in the compartment – to help her shell them. We were in fits of giggles from the beginning to the end of our trip.'

Elsy Jacobs died of cancer, shortly before her 65th birthday, in 1998. There's an annual cycling festival named after her in Garnich, which features a UCI 2.1 category women's race in her honour.

After Elsy's world championship victory, Luxembourg introduced a women's championship, which she won 15 times. © Presse Sports/Offside

BERYL BURTON

'Beryl the Peril'

'I hope it will not seem immodest of me to say so, but quite honestly I have lost count of all the medals I have won in my career,' Beryl Burton once wrote. It wasn't only Burton who struggled to keep a tally of her triumphs in the course of her more than 30-year racing career. 'How many races she won in total, nobody has yet calculated; it may have been close to a thousand', reckons British cycling historian Peter Whitfield.

How do you describe Burton's achievements without resorting to empty sounding hyperbole? For a quarter of a century, she roamed the land setting records and then shattering them, year in, year out. She was not only the strongest woman, but quite often stronger than the men. Many would argue she was the greatest ever female rider. And yet, in all other respects, she was really quite normal; a Yorkshire 'housewife' who cooked meals for her husband and daughter, kept the house in ship shape, held down a day job, did a bit of knitting in what spare time she had and, for a special treat, would go to the opera from time to time in Leeds.

Burton should be a feminist icon, the Billie Jean King of cycling. Presumably, though, she didn't need feminism; she already knew she was superior to most men. When she passed them in time trials, she would come out with some quip to remind them who was boss, like the classic, 'eh, lad, you're not trying'. If you've ever been locked in an argument with someone who claims that women's cycling doesn't merit the oxygen of media coverage that the men's sport gets, and that the reason for this is that women are weaker, and therefore less interesting or meritorious, Beryl is your trump card.

Take her mythic 12-hour time trial, which she rode in 1967. Having started out behind 99 men she spent the next 12 hours inexorably overtaking them all until there was only one man left, Mike McNamara, who was well on his way to cracking a British men's record of 9 years' standing. It was his greatest performance in a hugely impressive career. She passed him too, offering him a liquorice allsort to soften the blow – 'ta, love', he's said to have replied – before she powered on to smash both the women's and men's records in one of the hardest time trial categories there is. She rode 277.25 miles, climbing off her bike 45 seconds before the 12 hours were over, because she felt she'd done enough. It took two years for a man to beat Burton's distance.

It took a further 50 years and the advantages of a full kit of aerodynamic paraphernalia – carbon bike, disk wheel, tri bars, streamlined helmet and a skin suit – for a woman to do the same. This wasn't the only instance of Beryl beating the men. In fact, it was a fairly common event in the mid to late 1960s – and not just in some half-bit time trial out in the back of beyond – but in prestigious events, such as the British 100 mile championships in 1966, where she beat the winner of the men's championship, held a few weeks earlier on the same course, by 38 seconds. As one young male club rider put it in a TV documentary from 1986: 'You only ever see one view of her and that's a rear view. She goes by.'

Since we're on the subject of national championships, this is the moment to mention she won 96 national titles. That's right: 96. She was British road race champion a record 12 times, British 3,000m pursuit champion 13 times, and, in time trials, won pretty much every distance and category there was, from 10 through to 100 miles. Well, your friend who thinks female cyclists don't warrant TV time might argue, the competition in national championships was probably weak and all she had to do was train for a few races in the year. So now let's consider an award that in time-trialling circles in Britain holds more prestige than winning a national championship; the BAR, or Best All Rounder competition, given to the rider with the highest average speed, calculated to three decimal points, based on their best results in the course of the year over 25-, 50- and 100-mile distances. (The men's BAR gets calculated on their best 50-mile, 100-mile and 12-hour results.)

To win the BAR you have to be at the top of your game throughout the season. You can never rest easy, because any exceptional time you post will be under attack from your rivals the following week. Burton won the BAR award 25 years in succession. It goes without saying that no one else has come even remotely close to such an achievement. OK, your friend will say, these BAR records are only relevant within an island community featuring amateurs working full-time jobs with only part-time training opportunities. It's how she compared internationally that really counts. So let's take a look at that.

In the 25-year period during which Burton utterly dominated her sport, the only prestigious international races in which female cyclists could compete were the world championships, which had been introduced in 1958, on the road and on the track. Burton won seven world championship gold medals out of a total haul of 15 in two completely different disciplines; two in the road race, and five in the 3,000m pursuit on the track (without, incidentally, having a velodrome to train on at home). The world championships did not introduce time trials, Burton's great forte, until 1994. Had they existed in her time, there is no doubt that she would have doubled, if not tripled, her collection of rainbow jerseys.

But your 'friend', if you haven't throttled him yet, is still insisting all these results mean nothing compared to what the pros (meaning male riders) achieved. He'll be sitting there gleefully rubbing his hands, knowing you've got no response, because there are no races in which women can ride against the men. So we'll never know.

Only, in Beryl's case, there is in fact an answer to that too, because in 1968 she got to ride in the *Grand Prix des Nations,* which at the time was the de facto World Championship of time trialling. Held outside Paris, the *Nations'* previous winners included Fausto Coppi, Hugo Koblet and Jacques Anquetil – who'd won it a record 9 times. Thanks to a bit of networking by the English cycling journalist, Jock Wadley, Burton ended up being invited to take part.

She had to ride it ahead of the men, and she wasn't allowed to appear on the final classification, but for a couple of hours one Sunday afternoon, she got to ride the world's top time trial, against the best men in the world, with all the trimmings – including a police escort and roadside fans. Wadley told the French press beforehand that he thought she could manage the 73.5km course at a speed of 40km/h. In the end she exceeded everyone's expectations by riding a shade under 42km/h, with an average speed of 41.853km/h.

> She had to ride it ahead of the men, and she wasn't allowed to appear on the final classification.

The time trial finished in a velodrome on the outskirts of Paris. While the crowds waited for the champions, track riders entertained them with a series of exhibition races. Wadley was following Burton out on the course and judging from the astonished looks on policemen's faces, he realised no one was expecting her to come through so soon. Putting two and two together, he drove ahead to warn the organisers to clear the track, but no one paid him any heed. And so Burton arrived, well ahead of schedule, slap bang in the middle of another race. She completed her ride, which was supposed to feature two loops of the track, but, since the official timekeepers weren't ready, turned into three, with the other riders circling at the top of the steep banking.

So how did she compare to the men? She was only one minute slower than the last rider and 12 minutes slower than the winner, Felice Gimondi, who was one of the best riders in the world and had set a new course record. She finished only eight minutes down on Luis Ocaña, who would become one of Eddy Merckx's greatest adversaries. One French journalist noted that had the amateur men been taking part, she would have beaten eight of them based on their previous year's performances.

This Yorkshire housewife, who had never received a penny in sponsorship, or any professional coaching, who could train only part-time in between working

132 Beryl Burton

on a rhubarb farm and looking after her husband and child, rode a game of cat and mouse against the some of the best, professionally paid, technically and domestically supported time trial experts – men who could devote themselves entirely to training, racing and recovering: and still no-one could catch her.

How the hell did she manage it?

Perhaps the most remarkable thing about Beryl Burton was in fact how unlikely it was that she became a cyclist in the first place. As a child she had suffered a traumatic experience that would affect her for the rest of her life. As a young girl she was a good, conscientious student, who enjoyed learning. Then she sat down for the 11+ exam that would decide her academic future. Her mind went completely blank. All she knew, when she walked out of the exam, was that she had completely failed in the most humiliating way.

Burton would later describe what followed as a nervous breakdown; she was rushed into hospital with rheumatic fever and chorea, an illness triggering involuntary muscle spasms and twitching. It must have been terrifying: she had to spend nine months in hospital, and a further 15 in a convalescent home. For a long time she was partially paralysed and unable to speak properly. Rheumatic fever often results in damage to the heart, and when she finally returned home she was told in no uncertain terms that she had to take it easy from henceforth. In other words: no sport.

Her first job on leaving school was in the office of the Leeds-based tailor, Sir Montagu Burton. 'One day a bronzed-looking chap came into the office and attracted my attention immediately', she later wrote. 'I eyed him from top to bottom without, I hoped, making it too obvious. When my eyes alighted on his feet I thought "Oh dear, the poor chap must have something wrong with them." In fact he was wearing cycling shoes, which I had never seen before.'

Charlie Burton (who bore no relation to the company's founder) clearly took a liking to Beryl too, and before long was lending her one of his bikes, and not long after that, had talked her into joining *Morley CC,* his local cycling club, where she would join him on the Sunday club rides. The Yorkshire Dales offer spectacular, but unforgiving, cycling terrain. Even if the start of the ride was pleasantly downhill, 'The rest of the day usually remained a blank. I would return home absolutely whacked', Beryl recalled. 'For weeks mother would ask me on my return home where I had been and usually I had no idea.' Beryl was by no means an overnight cycling sensation. As Charlie later said, 'First of all, she was handy but wasn't that competent: we used to have to push her round a bit. Slowly she got better. By the second year, she was one of the lads and could ride with us. By the third year, she was going out in front and leading them all.'

Beryl and Charlie married shortly before she turned 18, and a year later their daughter, Denise, was born. By this time Beryl had started riding in local time trials, and was enjoying racing. Charlie bought a sidecar for Denise and the Burtons continued their club rides, while Charlie's mother helped look after the baby so that Beryl could train and race. The young family went everywhere by bike, even going on touring holidays with Denise.

Around this time Beryl started working for another rider in the club, Nim Carline, who had a rhubarb farm. Burton would spend all day working on Carline's farm, and then train with him after work. The farm labour was backbreaking and Carline treated Burton no differently to his male employees, but the training was even tougher. Carline was, in fact, another legend of Yorkshire cycling, whose speciality was the 24-hour time trial, in which he would eventually become a six-time national champion. He was also a keen mountaineer, who climbed in the Cairngorms, the Alps and later, the Himalayas.

'He was such a hard taskmaster that I would wait in the house before a training run wishing that there was some way I could avoid it', she later recalled. 'I was in and out of the lavatory and perspiring even before I sat on the bike. There was no question of simply following him. I had to match him side by side, although toward the end of the stint I just had to follow his wheel, tears in my eyes, but determined that I would not drop behind.' Burton would always insist that it was these gruelling training sessions that turned her into the crushingly powerful rider she became. Indeed, she never considered herself to have an exceptional natural talent, rather she felt it was her willingness to suffer, and to push herself to extremes, that gave her the upper hand. Her breakout season came in 1958 when she won not only her first, but her first three national titles, in the 25-, 50- and 100-mile time trials.

> Later it would become a habit for her to break a record every time she won a national title.

Later it would become a habit for her to break a record every time she won a national title. She would become the first woman to ride 25 miles in under an hour, the first to ride 50 miles in under two hours, the first woman to ride 100 miles in less than 4½ hours, and then the first to ride 100 in under four hours, a time which, for male riders alone, had had the same mythic quality as Roger Bannister running a mile in under four minutes, and which had only been cracked by Ray Booty in 1956, at the start of Burton's cycling career. It was simply inconceivable at that point that a woman could ride that fast.

The 1958 season also marked the last year Burton encountered a serious rival capable of consistently beating her. The year was dominated by a protracted duel with her friend Millie Robinson, who broke several records herself in the

Herne Hill Champions Meeting 1969. © Colorsport/REX/Shutterstock

course of the year and finally became that year's BAR, having come second the two previous seasons.

By 1959 Beryl was flying, winning the first of her 25 BAR awards and her first world championship gold medal, in the 3,000m individual pursuit against the Luxembourg rider and defending road race champion, Elsy Jacobs, in Liège. Despite being so nervous going into the final that she couldn't lace up her cycling shoes, she managed to pull out all the stops when it mattered. 'My competitive urge came to the top and I sought some kind of retribution against the gods for that damned 11-plus and the childhood ill-health', she later wrote. The same year she also won the first of her British national road race championships.

Her strength, however, was also her greatest weakness in road racing, which rewards the crafty. She had no tactics. She just had one technique, and that was to crush the opposition. She would attack early and never be seen again, or she'd set such a high pace that her rivals would explode one by one in her wake. Her Achilles heel was that she had no sprint. In her autobiography she describes at least three world championship races where she considered herself the 'moral victor'. She would spend the entire race 'towing' the lead riders around the course, who would refuse to share the burden of pacemaking and then outsprint her at the finish.

Beryl and Denise 1971. Charlie is in the middle. © John Knoote/REX/Shutterstock

Could she have raced smarter with more support? There was no science to her training, which was simply to ride long, and hard. The British Cycling Federation didn't offer coaches or training camps. Riders weren't drilled on tactics. Indeed, budgets were so minimal, riders had to subsidise their attendance at the worlds, whether that meant covering their travel expenses or bringing their own spare parts. Charlie would cross Alpine passes on the back of a friend's tiny motor scooter and sleep in tents in order to provide Beryl with the support she needed.

Bernadette Malvern (née Swinnerton) who came from a large Stoke-on-Trent cycling dynasty, recalls a race much later in Burton's career, when she was 'with a group of girls who she could not shake off. They just refused to be dropped so she jammed on her brakes and caused a crash behind her.' Her bitterness about sprinters erupted most famously in terrible public spat with her daughter, Denise.

Denise had started racing as a teenager, and in the early 1970s grew into a formidable talent in her own right – she was even selected for the Great Britain team at the age of only 14. For quite a few years they took part in the same races, and so it was that in the 1976 road race national championships they both ended up in a small lead group, featuring one other rider, Carol Barton. In the final sprint, Denise prevailed against her mum. On the podium, Beryl refused to shake her daughter's hand, and the event made headlines the following day. 'It was not a sporting thing to do', Burton later wrote, 'I can only plead that I was not myself at the time.' 'I had worked very hard all my life, and fitted in my racing and training with a job as well as the household work', she explained. 'Rightly or wrongly I felt there were times when Denise could do more, and that Charlie did not support my point of view.'

British newspapers – which had previously given only cursory coverage of her extraordinary world championship gold medals and other achievements – now had a field day, portraying her as a terrible mother, so obsessed with winning she was incapable of celebrating her daughter's triumph. And perhaps she was a bit monstrous. 'She tried to psych me out right from the beginning', Denise recalls of that race. 'When it came to getting in the car to go to Harrogate, she wouldn't let me in. So I said, "how am I supposed to get there?" and she said, "you'll have to ride", so I said, "you can at least take my bags then". So she let my bags go in the car but she wouldn't let my wheels go in. I had to put on those little gadgets that you fit across your spindle and your spare wheels can go on the front. I had to ride out to Harrogate from where we lived which was about 25 miles, maybe 20. I just thought, oh well, it's a good warm-up. I rode out and then apparently when my dad dropped her off everyone said, "where's Denise?" and he just turned around and picked me up.' Denise says they never talked about what happened. They just got on with their lives, like they always did. 'I had beaten her before in road races and pursuits, but it was a national championships, and it was in *Yorkshire*. That was the difference.' When I ask

Denise whether Beryl ever gave her any racing advice, it takes a moment before she can think of anything, finally remembering her mum reminding her to always have one rest day in the week. Another time she initiated her on the steep banking of a velodrome by getting her to follow her round. As for everything else, Denise was left to work things out on her own. 'We never trained together. Never. She was encouraging for my racing and congratulatory up until I started being a rival.'

It wasn't long before Denise moved out, and married a rider from another club.

> 'Why can't I just go home and be like other people and go out for the day in the car up to the Dales or something like that?'

Despite receiving offers to turn professional, Beryl remained an amateur throughout her career. Riding at such a high level naturally came at a cost, however, and most of her salary went on her equipment and expenses. For a long time the family couldn't afford a car and Beryl would ride to or from races on the other side of the country as a way of saving money and getting more training in. When she and Charlie were invited to end-of-season parties held by cycling clubs, they would ride across Yorkshire and Lancashire to attend dinners in the middle of winter, 'arriving home in time to meet the milkman'.

Peter Whitfield, in his book *12 Champions*, talks of her riding over 100 miles to visit a journalist who needed to do an extended interview with her, then riding back the following morning. On another occasion, she rode some 200 miles to a club dinner in London, then rode home at 6am the following morning. 'She didn't notice when the A1 became the A1M, until a police patrol ordered her off the motorway', he writes.

Beryl had a reputation for being down to earth and friendly, a rider without airs and graces who treated all cyclists as equals. Yet behind that easy going demeanour was a rider caught up in the grip of an almost terrifying determination. Winning became an addiction, one she could not withstand, even when her health suffered. Only two goals eluded her and caused her any regret; her unsuccessful attempt to break the hour record in Milan, which in retrospect can only be blamed on bad luck and a lack of time and resources, and a failed attempt at a 24-hour time trial because of a knee injury. It's quite possible, had the knees held out, that this ride would have surpassed even her achievements in the mythic 12-hour, since with the times and distances she was clocking, she was set to explode the 496.3 mile record her training partner and mentor, Nim Carline, had set in 1966.

'From a riding point of view I was in good shape and in no way distressed [...] But the pain from my knees was just too much', Burton later wrote. 'I climbed into the car with the veins behind my knees looking like plastic tubes and I

could not bear to touch them myself, let alone allow anyone else to do so.' The eventual winner, Roy Cromack, set a new record of 507 miles. 'Without that knee problem, would Beryl have topped 500 miles and beaten Cromack?' writes Whitfield. 'Looking at the way she was riding, you would have to say yes: but you would also have to say that no sensible person would even have started that particular race.' Later in her career Burton suffered a series of terrible crashes, yet fought against pain and doctors' advice to defend titles or maintain her BAR standing. There was never any question of pulling out of a race, even if she was ill and knew she had no chance of winning. She would wade into battle regardless, and fight till the bitter end. On one occasion she rode a track world championship race with an injured hand strapped to the handlebar. The pain had made her fingers numb, so she couldn't keep the bike upright. That determination applied to her career too. Beryl simply couldn't stop. There was always another record to break, a title to defend, a new tally with a catchy round number to achieve. She became asthmatic, then anaemic. Her doctors begged her to stop riding, yet even when she 'retired' from competing for the BAR award, she still couldn't stop chasing other victories. Perhaps the void of not having a race to win was too frightening to contemplate.

Asked in a TV interview in 1986, when she was 49, whether she enjoyed winning, she said, 'not when I'm actually on the bike and I'm striving to win. Not now. I'll think, "God, what on earth am I doing here? *Why* am I doing this?" And yet the bit's between my teeth and I'm eyeballs hanging over the front wheel and I'm really giving it 100%. Yet I think: "why can't I just go home and be like other people and go out for the day in the car up to the Dales or something like that?" It's just this will to win and this determination to be number one. And you don't know when it will go out – I may have it for another 20 years!' she added, with a rueful laugh. As it happened, her body gave up first. Burton died ten years later, while out riding her bike, delivering invitations to her 59th birthday. Her heart, it seems, simply packed in. She had planned to take part in a 10-mile time trial the following week.

During her life Burton received many honours, including an OBE and an MBE yet she was always frustrated by the lack of recognition she received in the press, not just for herself, but for the sport. After becoming double world champion in Leipzig in 1960, Beryl came home, as usual, to a few cursory mentions in the national and local press. 'It might as well have been the ladies' darts final down at the local as far as Britain was concerned.'

I like to imagine Beryl's ghost haunting the Yorkshire landscape. Our friend, who doesn't think much of women's racing, will be on a lonely road in the moors at dusk, grinding his way up a difficult incline, when another rider will silently overtake: too fast, in the grey light, for him to tell whether it's a man or a woman. All he'll really notice is the bent back, still and powerful, the fluid motion of the muscular legs spinning a huge gear, the old-fashioned steel frame, the silvery gleam of box-section wheel rims. As he sprints to catch up, this rider simply surges on with the same ease as if he or she were ticking off laps in a velodrome. Our friend will redouble his efforts, but he can only watch helplessly as the other rider, smooth as silk, disappears into the gathering gloom.

And then – did he hear that or imagine it? A voice in his ear: 'eh lad, you're not trying.'

Beryl racing in North Yorkshire on a Ron Kitching bike, made in Harrogate. © Brian Townsley

'Belgium's First Lady'

Yvonne Reynders had the face of an angel and rode like the devil.

In road races she was merciless. 'I would attack, let everyone catch up with me, then attack again. I could keep on doing this again and again until I killed them. It was easy', she says, matter of factly. Sometimes she rode in a fury, punching the pedals in rage at her boastful, hard-drinking, philandering stepdad. He'd be there at the races, a huge man both in girth and height, yelling and cursing, ever-ready to bask in his daughter's glory, yet quite unwilling to change a wheel or pump up a tire. Those races she won because and in spite of him.

Reynders had no weaknesses: she could sprint, climb, time-trial, launch blistering accelerations, withstand cobbles and great distances. She excelled on both the road and on the track. With her appetite for winning everything, she was the Eddy Merckx of women's racing. She even resembled him, strangely. Not so much in her features, but in a certain expression of cool focus and merciless self-confidence you can sometimes catch in photos, usually just before a race.

Just look at her face at the start of a sprint, the strangest and perhaps most exciting of track disciplines to watch, a game of psychological warfare in which a rider tries to unnerve, intimidate or trick her opponent into making a false move so that she can accelerate into the sprint with enough of fractional advantage to win. You don't need a race report to know who won. Yvonne gazes assertively at the camera, the picture of insolent self-assurance, while her rival seems to have fallen apart before the race has even begun.

Beryl Burton, who always made a point of being friendly to her rivals, would later write about Reynders' 'glazed' expression in between events when they competed on the track. She would be aloof, inscrutable behind her mask, one of the few riders with whom Burton could never connect.

It's early January and I've come to Belgium to meet Yvonne. I've taken the train to Antwerp, then a 40-minute bus ride east of the city. The weather is filthy; cold and wet with the sort of heavy grey skies that make you feel like the day is over at 11am. Yvonne has told me to meet her at a local hotel, and at 2pm on the dot she rocks up with a posse of four friends, one of whom, Maurice Hermans, authored her biography. Two others are here to help translate. The fourth is introduced as a girlfriend she shared a house with for 15 years. We start out with coffees – before swiftly moving onto glasses of Tripel.

She's still instantly recognisable with her pleasant oval features, neat nose and clear blue eyes. She jokes in her husky, slightly nasal Flemish that she has more wrinkles on the left side of her face because she always turned that way when she raced. She comes across as supremely capable, like a woman who'd know how to fix a car in a blizzard, or catch a giant pike.

Yvonne was born in 1937 in Schaerbeek, a suburb South of Brussels, but grew up in Antwerp where her parents were coal dealers. When Yvonne left school at the age of 15 she was given a cargo bike and set to work delivering coal.

The coal came in 10-kilo sacks, which she would carry up to people's apartments, sometimes as high as the 7th floor, in buildings without lifts. She started out with a sack in each hand, but soon got bored running up and down stairs all the time.

Yvonne could deliver up to 250 kilos of coal on her bike. © Yvonne Reynders

So she tried putting a couple of sacks on her back and a sack in one hand. The staircases were in a narrow spiral formation, so she had to go up sideways at an awkward angle. Finally she carried three sacks on her back, one under her arm and the other in her hand: 50 kilos in total.

Yvonne's bike was supposed to be able to carry 200 kilos, but she would pack it with 250. Sometimes the pedals broke, or a wheel. She kept a spare cargo bike for such eventualities.

Yvonne would do this work from 8am until 9.30pm in winter, six days a week, lifting 1,000 kilos and cycling about 40km a day, in and around the cobbled streets of Antwerp. In the summer she would finish work around 5pm. When she took up racing later, she would use the shorter summer working days to jump on her road bike and do a 140km training ride in the evenings.

She did this for about four or five years and only stopped delivering coal when she became world champion.

Unsurprisingly, the coal deliveries made her immensely strong. She took up athletics and instantly excelled in discuss, shot-put and javelin, winning her first competition with only two weeks' practice. When she was 17 she became the national junior discuss champion, a title she held for three consecutive years. During the same period she also won two silver medals and a bronze in javelin and shot-put.

One day her mother read in the paper that women's bike races were being reintroduced. Yvonne joked with her about how she would win those too.
A local lad overheard the conversation and went home and told his dad.
That evening his father turned up at their door with a bike; 'I heard you're talking about racing bikes now. Why don't you take mine and have a go.'

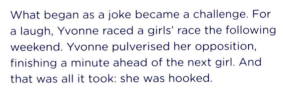

What began as a joke became a challenge. For a laugh, Yvonne raced a girls' race the following weekend. Yvonne pulverised her opposition, finishing a minute ahead of the next girl. And that was all it took: she was hooked.

The first races Yvonne took part in were criteriums. These were organised by pubs and would feature a 3km circuit around a church. The races were usually about 70km long so the pubs could sell as much beer as possible to the raucous, appreciative crowd, which got plenty of opportunity to ogle the young women's legs as they went round.

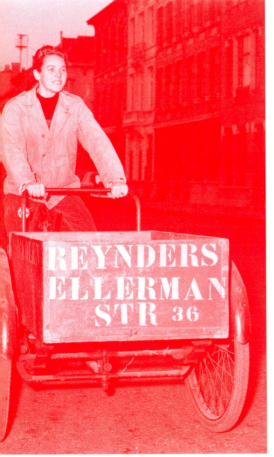

Not that this was some pretty girls' parade. The races were technically hard, with unrelenting cobbles, sharp corners, pavements, potholes, gutters and tram tracks to negotiate at high speed in a bunch. Finally there were the other riders; a generation of mercenary women who bolted off right from the start. If you weren't part of the initial explosion, you might as well give up and go home.

Out of this scene came a number of great Belgian riders who would also play a dominating role in the world championship road race, like Rosa Sels (silver medallist in 1960 and 1963 and bronze in 1964) and Marie-Rose Gaillard, who led a clean sweep of the podium in 1962, with Yvonne Reynders in second place and Marie-Thérèse Naessens, an ever present rival, in third.

Women's racing in the 1950s was a chaotic affair though. The Belgian cycling federation didn't acknowledge women's races when Yvonne started out, and the three 'national championships' she won in 1956, 1957 and 1958 do not appear in official histories.

Finally in 1958 Yvonne's stepfather, Maurice Van de Vyver, set up a Belgian Women's Cycling Federation to help protect their interests and promote their races. In this way Belgian women were able to obtain UCI licences so that they could race in the first women's world championships that same year in Reims.

When I ask her about him, Yvonne insists their relations were 'normal', but that's not what she's said in past interviews with the Belgian press. She has claimed he married her mother bigamously, that he drank and had such a terrible temper that she always hid in her room when he came home from the pub. He didn't take proper care of her mother who suffered from tuberculosis and to whom she was very close. She has said that despite having several suitors she refused to marry because of the terrible example he set. She said he never once helped her with her bikes, yet was quite happy to boast incessantly about her abilities to the other riders and their fathers. Her rivals, annoyed by his bragging, would unite against her in races. Once, when she confronted him about it, they got into such a row she ended up throwing her bike down the cellar steps.

Reynders was not only strong but crafty, a cunning mercenary and race tactician.

Yvonne learnt very early not to rely on anyone. She found her first racing bike at a local scrap dealer. After that, she always built up her own frames, even when she could get them custom made. Bike manufacturers would be surprised when she turned up to supervise their work. On one occasion when they had finished welding the frame, she took it home during their lunch break and painted it herself. 'I got my mum to hold the frame – unfortunately she got covered with paint!' she laughs. When she brought it back to the factory, she astonished everyone by assembling all the parts herself. 'I never let anyone lay a finger on my bikes', she says.

She was perhaps the greatest road racer of her generation, the rare woman in whom Burton met her match at the world championships in both the road race and the individual pursuit on the track. They were perfect rivals, each winning seven gold medals. Born the same year, they were titanesses of their sport and largely unbeaten in their own countries. The gold medal would go back and forth between them from one year to the next, each pushing the other to her limits. In her autobiography Burton describes her searingly difficult 1963 pursuit win against a 'jet-propelled' Reynders as the 'pinnacle' of her pursuiting career, more impressive even than her victory the previous year in Milan in which she broke the mythical four-minute barrier.

Unlike Burton, however, who won races by burning out her opposition with a sustained, relentlessly high pace, Reynders was not only strong but crafty, a cunning mercenary and race tactician.

Their divergent talents were also reflected in their world championship gold medals; the majority of Burton's medals were in the 3,000m pursuit, which is essentially a form of time trial, and only two of her golds were on the road. Reynders on the other hand won four in the much less predictable road race – and three on the track.

She won her first world championship in 1959, on home turf in Belgium. Before the race she'd been told that the English always rode on the left-hand side of the road, and that everyone would follow them, so she attacked on the right and took everyone by surprise. As confusion reigned behind, Reynders came across a Belgian policeman on a motorbike escorting the race. When he realised he had a Belgian medal contender right behind, he drafted her some of the way to the finish.

She says one of her proudest achievements was winning both the individual pursuit and the road race at the world championships on the Isle of Man in 1961. She'd already beaten defending champion Beryl Burton in the pursuit, and now Burton was seeking revenge – and to defend her title – in the road race. Reynders had brought two bikes, a fancy new racing frame, and a cheaper, much heavier, spare. The race took place on the Willaston circuit, a not particularly easy route, as Burton later described it: 'Its forty corners required plenty of braking action, particularly the corner in Onchan which I never liked; it needed a fast approach followed by vicious braking, then immediately a hill. It was a killer on the legs, and called for some slick gear-changing.' Halfway through the race Reynders' brake cable snapped and she had to swap bikes. When she made it back to the bunch she learnt there was a breakaway up ahead containing Burton, Elsy Jacobs – the 1958 world champion – and a couple of Russians. There was nothing for it but to bridge the gap, which she did, in what Burton later called, 'a superb piece of riding'. At this point Burton and Jacobs promptly instructed her to take her turn at the front. 'Sorry,' Yvonne said, 'but I've had to fight my way back to the bunch, and then jump over to you. There's no way I can take a pull right now.' They continued riding, and after a while Burton and Jacobs' calls for help became more insistent. 'All right if you want me to ride, I'll

Roller stunts to earn some extra cash while her stepfather looks on. © Yvonne Reynders

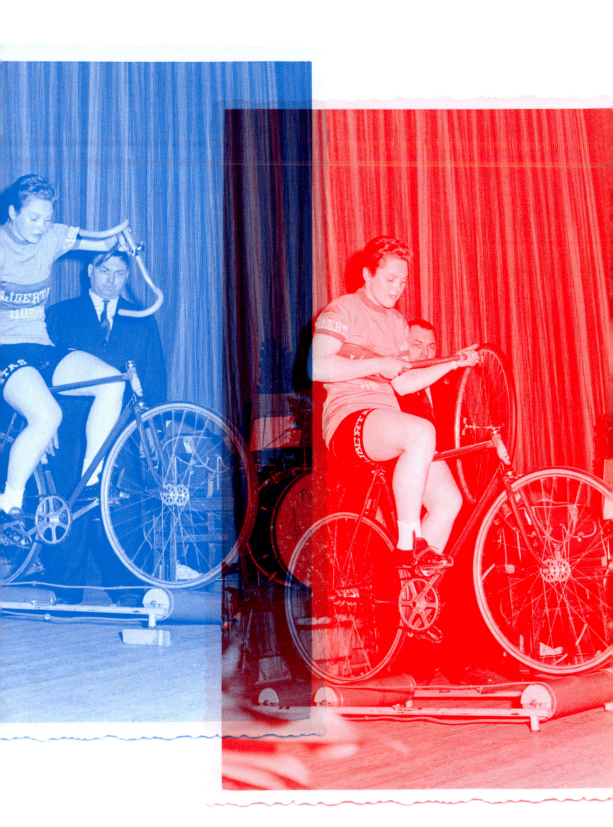

do exactly that', thought Reynders, and with that she rode off, all the way to the finish, with Burton and Jacobs, having to settle for second and third.

On another occasion Reynders was encouraged by her friend Lyli Herse to take part in the *Trophée de Grimpeurs*, a race for climbers on a hilly circuit outside Paris.

Reynders was thinking about catching the train home, so broke away early and started to ride hard so she could get to the station in time. After a while she heard some riders coming up behind. When she turned to take a look, she discovered it wasn't her rivals coming back to get her, but six men with Raymond Poulidor in their midst. She had ridden her way into the men's edition of the race, which used the same route but started at a different time. As the men attacked the next steep climb, they discovered they couldn't shake her off. At some point the race commissaire's car came along and started calling through a loudhailer for her to get out of the men's way. Yvonne refused, however, and the men backed her up, protecting her all the way up to the top of the hill. It was only on the descent that she finally dropped back; too light to descend at the same speed.

Reynders is a born raconteur. It's getting late and our interview has turned into a party, of which she's the life and soul. The beers and anecdotes are flowing. When Yvonne tells a story, it starts out slowly, then builds momentum. She'll do voice impressions and sound effects. She'll gesticulate, get up from the table and roam around the room acting out the different characters' parts as tears of laughter roll down her friends' faces. After about 10 minutes of mirth, I get a three sentence précis, told as fast as possible so as not to miss the next story that's bubbling up.

When I ask if she ever trained with male riders – Rik Van Steenbergen was a friend and a member of the same club – she ends up telling a story about going for a training ride with a friend, and how they'd both run out of water and gone into a shop which could only offer them wine to drink. So they shared a bottle of wine and set off down the road again. After a bit they were no longer holding such a straight line and a police car started to tail them. 'Can I see your identity card?' asks the police officer, and Yvonne reluctantly produces hers. 'Ah, I see you're Yvonne Reynders!' he declares – for at this point she is a celebrity. 'Ah no, that's my sister!' she protests. The police officer isn't fooled however. 'I'll tell you what, I won't give you a fine if you ride from here to the next village without dropping below 40km an hour. That way we'll know if you're really sober or not.' Naturally, Yvonne lived up to the challenge. Many years later she was standing in a crowd watching a race when someone tapped on her shoulder. 'Do you recognise me?' asked the man. 'I'm the policeman who stopped you all those years ago!'

There's a ten-year break in Reynder's palmares which starts in 1967 when she failed a dope test. She has always vigorously denied that she cheated. In one interview she pointed out that the test took place in Holland just before the world championships, and that all the other women who failed were Belgian, too much of a coincidence, she said, when their arch rivals were hosting the race on home turf. Reynders was given a three-month suspension, effective immediately. Her response was to walk away from the sport.

She still insists on her innocence. At some point in our interview she tells me about her phenomenally strong muscles, and how she'd been sent to the local hospital for testing at one point since everyone assumed she must be doping. The doctors declared her muscles were so uncommonly strong, that she should on no account do any strength training if she didn't want to permanently damage her bones.

Ten years later, she made a surprise come back, winning the Belgian national championship and coming third in the world championship world race, at the age of 39.

Despite her many victories, Reynders never made much money from racing – certainly not enough to live off. She became a podiatrist at one point, then a nurse, looking after patients with dementia. She often worked nights so she could train during the day. During the winter she would earn extra cash by doing exhibitions on rollers, performing stunts like removing the handlebars off her bike whilst riding it, then taking off a pair of tracksuit bottoms, fixing a puncture on a wheel and doing any number of awkward tasks, pedalling all the while.

These days Reynders lives on her own with her 27 exotic turtles and 8 chickens. She does a lot of fishing. She's an honorary citizen of Zoersel and is celebrated in the Flemish cycling museum in Roeselare. The R.A.B.C club, Belgium's oldest cycling club, celebrated both its 135th anniversary and her 80th birthday by presenting her with a special jersey with the words: 'Yvonne: Onze First Lady.' *Yvonne: Our First Lady.*

Amsterdam track 1967. Yvonne channeled her natural strength and toughness into a crushing racing style. © Ron Kroon/Anefo/DNA

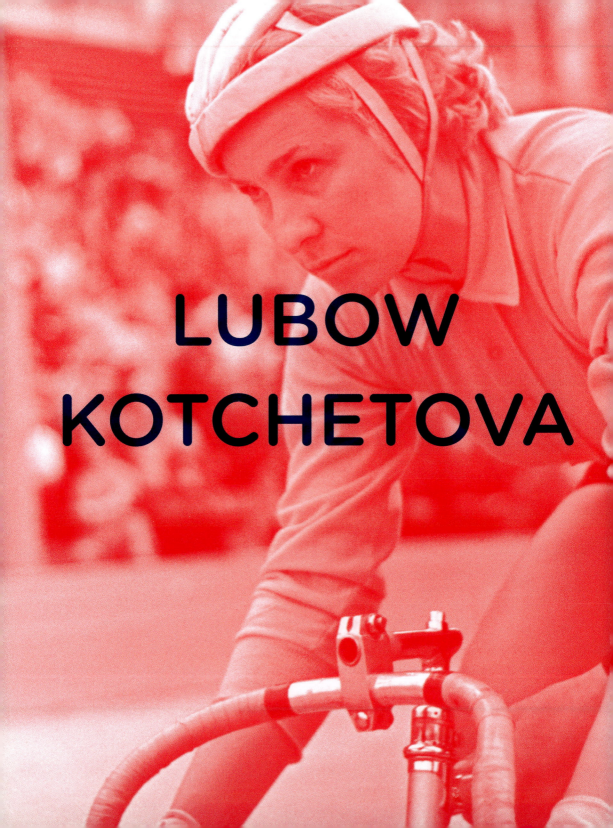

'Kotchetova and the Soviet Missiles'

It was a Wednesday evening in early September 1958 in Paris. Galina Ermolaeva and Valentina Maksimova had already taken the gold and silver in the world championship sprint finals. Tamara Novikova and Mariya Loukchina had taken silver and bronze in the road race earlier in the week. Now it was Lubow's turn in the 3,000m pursuit final.

At the Parc des Princes velodrome the floodlights were on the track. There was an end of summer nip in the air. It was just herself now, against the English rider Stella Bail. The low din of spectators in anticipation. The evening breeze brushed against the hairs on her arms. Cement track: good. An enthusiastic crowd. The crowd is important. You give, and they take. They give, and you take. She'd been watching the British riders. They were undoubtedly strong. And experienced. Pragmatic and businesslike.

'Bail was the strongest, everybody thought she would win', says Marina Kotchetova, Lubow's daughter. 'My mother had to use a psychological trick. Everyone is different: some people start fast from the beginning. Some start slow and develop their speed. My mother usually started slowly and gradually increased her speed. She knew if she rode in her usual way it wouldn't work, because Bail probably also knew my mother usually speeded up later.' Ah yes, she had seen the British coach looking their way when they were training, stopwatch discreetly in hand. Everyone did it. Bail was a confident woman, always remonstrating with the officials. But Lubow was confident, too.

There was only really one option: fool Bail by going fast from the start. They had to hope the English woman would take the sensible approach and wait for Lubow to flag. The only problem with the Russian plan was that it was suicidal. She would have no choice but to persist at her lung-bursting pace if she wanted to win. The starter was getting them ready now. Lubow took a deep breath.

From 1958 when the women's world championships began, until the late 1970s, Russian women absolutely dominated international women's cycling. Though their greatest successes were on the track, with only three occasions between 1958 and 1978 in which a Soviet rider didn't win the sprint, they didn't do badly on the road either: between 1958 and 1974 Soviet riders only missed the podium three times.

Between 1967 and 1974 no one could get past Tamara Garkushina and Raisa Obodovskaya in the 3,000m pursuit.

'We expect to win all the first prizes', they told the *Birmingham Post* with a smile, at the 1961 world championships on the Isle of Man. They would come to races, conquer, and then leave, and no one made friends with them or got to know them. The greatest, strongest champions in the West met their match against these mysterious, often beautiful, frequently tough-looking women with colossal thighs and unpronounceable names. They were so strong, many Western riders automatically assumed they were cheating. The British track sprint specialist Bernadette Malvern recalls how the Russians, 'were romping away winning everything', at her first world championships in Rome in 1968. 'And the size of them! You just didn't trust that they were being straight, because of the way they looked. You just thought, "how can anybody develop their body like that naturally?" And how can they turn such fantastically enormous gears? I couldn't believe it at all.'

> 'You just thought, "how can anybody develop their body like that naturally?"'

Who were these riders, where did they come from and what made them so dominant?

Lubow Kotchetova's story is one of many Russian riders' stories. She was part of the first wave of Russians to win on the international stage in 1958, and she later became a national coach, whose protégés included the phenomenal pursuit specialist, Tamara Garkushina, who not even the great Beryl Burton could beat. Her tale is indicative of the long journey many of these riders took, before they had even boarded the Aeroflot plane on the Moscow airport tarmac.

Lubow – whose first name means 'love' in Russian – was born in the town of Borisov in Belarus, at the time part of the USSR, on 12 July 1929. Her family moved to Leningrad – as St Petersburg was then called – when she was a baby, after her father had been made responsible for coordinating the supply of all shoes to the city's shops.

In recognition of this high-status role, Lubow's family was installed in a palatial apartment block erected during the time of Peter the Great. It had high ceilings and vast rooms and had once been a luxury hotel. Each family was allocated one room. A long corridor connected the five or six rooms on each floor with a kitchen and a bathroom. The families devised schedules for when they could cook or wash.

Lubow was a lively, vivacious child. She loved accompanying her father on his work trips and trying on all the shoes. She liked to dance and act. She would spend hours in front of the grand mirror in the hallway practising her moves, imagining herself under the spotlight of the great Mariinsky Theatre stage. She was also a sickly child who was constantly ill as a result of the damp St Petersburg climate.

Lubow was 11 when the war broke out. On the very first day her father was sent away to the Front, and her brother, who was only 16 and officially too young to enlist, ran off and signed up anyway. In September 1941 German, Finnish and Spanish forces began a blockade that would last nearly two and half years. Directives to the German Army were simple: do not occupy the city and on no account accept a surrender, since that would entail a responsibility to feed the population. Hitler's plan was to starve the people of Leningrad to death, after which the city would be razed to the ground, as if it had never existed. What followed was one of the longest and most horrific sieges in history, in which an estimated 1,500,000 people died.

Daily life became an unimaginable hell. People died, constantly, everywhere. They simply collapsed in the street. There was no fuel with which to heat apartments, so families burnt their furniture, books and clothes to keep warm. Lubow's mother would boil leather belts and wood for food. One time the family received an onion. They cut it into six and shared each part with the other families on their floor. Another time a neighbour invited the children round to eat some meat. When Lubow learnt afterwards that they had eaten a cat she was violently sick.

One means of obtaining food was to help in the hospitals. The nurses had all been sent to the front so patients were looked after by volunteers. Lubow, aged 13, would try to sing and dance and tell jokes in an attempt to cheer up the wounded and dying. She tried to do the same thing in the market for food. A woman offered her three bars of chocolate in exchange for her coat. Lubow was so hungry she agreed. On her way home she discovered the chocolate was actually soap.

Her four-year-old brother died. Lubow's family was selected for evacuation. They simply walked out of their apartment because there was nothing to bring and nothing to safeguard. The only way in or out of the city was across Lake Ladoga, a route that was subject to constant German bombing raids. Lubow's family was put in a boat. The bombing started when they were out on the water and the boats all around them started to capsize. 'It was a nightmare. They didn't know what to do', says Marina. 'There was an old lady in the boat and she told them to make three signs of the cross. The girls hadn't been baptised, they had grown up in a Communist family, but they did what the old lady told them. There was nothing else they could do. "Don't be afraid", the old lady said, "God is with us."' They reached the shore and were put into cattle trucks which took them to the Urals bordering Siberia, more than 1,000km away. They were far

from the frontline, and there was more food, but Lubow's family were in pitiful shape, covered in sores and suffering from gum disease. They had no news of their father or brother. Her mother told them: 'We shall overcome this. We have no choice.'

When the blockade was over they returned to their empty flat. There was hardly anyone left. Those neighbours who had survived supported each other, like members of an extended family. Lubow's father died two months before the end of the war. Her brother survived and came home a hero. Her mother worked three or four jobs to supplement her meagre widow's pension. Life resumed some semblance of normality. Lubow continued with her studies, and enrolled at the Leningrad Institute of Theatre, Music and Cinema with the ambition of becoming an actress. She had fallen into cycling quite by accident in her second year of university, when she volunteered to represent her department in a bike race. She couldn't actually ride a bike, but the university was expected to field a team and since no one else wanted to do it, she thought she might as well have a go. She liked adventures.

She managed to get through the race somewhere in the middle of the pack, but was unable to stop at the end. 'Please help me!' she shouted, before coming to

a crash landing, much to everyone's amusement. The next thing she knew, she'd been put on the university's cycling team, and there was no longer any choice in the matter: she had to race.

In her next race she was given some tips by a local coach, who had seen her riding in the previous race and she finished second. The coach had seen enough to make up his mind. She had no technique, but her immense potential was evident. He suggested there and then that she transfer to the sports academy, where she would receive free, systematic training, food, a uniform and a bus pass. It was a very attractive proposition. Lubow found she enjoyed the experience of racing: the sensation of riding fast, the atmosphere of the race and the sense of putting on a performance for the appreciative crowd. It had a lot in common with acting.

Her mother and grandmother were horrified, however. Had she forgotten how sickly she had been as a child? Why throw away her artistic ambitions? In the end the coach had to talk her family into letting her change. 'A talent like this is a blessing', he told them and they finally relented. A new door opened onto an exciting new world, one that was alien to anything she had previously experienced in life, which is, of course, precisely what you want when you're a precocious 19-year-old.

> Lubow found she enjoyed the experience of racing: the sensation of riding fast, the atmosphere of the race

The coach turned out to be Nikolai Ivanovich Petrov, head of the department of cycling at the Lesgaft National State University of Physical Education, Sport and Health: an entire university in St Petersburg dedicated to sport. He was famous not only as a coach, but for his research, part of a generation of Russian sports scientists whose ideas are still relevant today. Under his guidance Lubow progressed with astonishing speed. 'Normally it takes an average of five years to become a master of sport,' Marina explains, 'but within a year my mother was already winning races or coming second or third.'

In 1949 she won her first national championship after only one year of training. To appreciate the significance of this you have to remember how vast The Soviet Union was: an empire of 15 republics with a population of well over 200 million. Every rider was part of a club and in order to represent the Soviet Union first of all you had to win your club's championships, then work your way up a series of local and regional races before becoming the best in your republic. For most riders, simply getting to this point was like winning a medal.

Whereas the norm with track racing is to specialise in one particular discipline, Lubow had an exceptional ability to excel in every type of race, whether it was the 3,000m individual pursuit or the sprint, the 500m standing start or the kilometre. She was selected for the national team and moved to Moscow, which offered the best training opportunities in the country, and was given her own apartment. In Moscow she rode for The Air Forces Club which was managed by Joseph Stalin's son, Vasily. Vasily had been made Commander of the Airforce of the Moscow Military District by Russian officials currying favour with his father and he thoroughly understood the power of his position, adopting 'Stalin', his father's *nom de plume,* as his own. He also managed the Air Forces Hockey team, most of whom died in a terrible plane crash in a snowstorm on the way to Sverdlovsk airport in 1950. Fearing his father's wrath, Vasily quickly replaced the team and hushed up reports of the accident so his father wouldn't hear about it. 'In many books people wrote about [Vasily] as a drinker', says Marina, 'but my mother said he was an easy going person. He treated everybody equally. He was passionate about cycling. He never drank in front of his team. He did his job and he knew what he was doing. Kotchetova was his pet.'

In Moscow she also met Evgeniy Kotchetov, a young track cyclist who was also a national champion. Evgeniy's calm disposition was the perfect foil for Lubow's sometimes fiery, determined personality. They married in 1950. They were a young, golden couple and world was their oyster.

Then they surprised everyone by moving to Tula, Evgeniy's hometown, a small city three hours' drive from Moscow famous for its arms industry and samovar manufacturing. It was also 'the capital of cycling' Marina says, boasting the oldest velodrome in Russia. In Tula, cycling was everything. A big track event would attract crowds, 'like it was the first night at the opera', says Marina. Tula not only had the audience, but the riders. Local talents who excelled on both the national and international stage included Galina Ermolaeva, Valentina Maksimova, Tamara Garkushina, Valentina Savina, Tamara Pilshikova, Sergei Tereshenkov, Vitaly Petrakov and Sergei Kopylov. 'In 1980 Tula was the only town in the Soviet Union in which five world champion cyclists lived,' says Marina.

For Lubow, accustomed to big city life and all the privileges of being a star, Tula was in many respects a backwater; moving there would be like settling for life in a village. But at the same time, there was the legendary track, and she had fallen in love with it. 'It's like ballet,' Marina explains, 'it's important which stage you are on. It's the same thing with cycling.'

In Tula, Lubow's career continued in the ascendant. She would eventually break 8 world records, win 16 Soviet Union national championships and 24 Russian national championships. Defying all conventional wisdom, however, she still refused to specialise in one particular discipline – she excelled at them all. In 1953, however, that particular decision was taken out of her hands.

She was at the national championships in Moscow and had already won the 3,000m pursuit and was in the final in the sprint. Lubow's rival was another young woman from Tula called Lubow Rasouvayeva. They were at top speed, in the final convulsive moment of the race when Rasouvayeva touched Lubow's wheel when she was least expecting it.. She lost control of her bike and came down hard, catapulted at high velocity onto the unforgiving concrete. She lay unconscious, her face drained of all colour. Blood began to trickle from her ears. Evgeniy could not revive her. Much later, at the hospital, he learned her skull was badly fractured and told to prepare for the worst: she would die within a week. Vasily Stalin himself worked the phones to get her the best doctors, but the city's top surgeons could only agree that her situation was hopeless.

And yet, defying everyone's expectations, Lubow did not die.

Life as she had known it, however, was over. She could barely talk, hear or recognise people. At one point the doctors had had to put needles in her spine and in the process had left her partially paralysed – for the next six months she would be confined to her bed or to wheel chairs, unable to move her legs. Evgeniy spent every spare moment looking after her, helping her with exercises but also doing what he could to boost her morale. Perhaps as an athlete he understood better than anyone the role of the mind in achieving the seemingly impossible. 'He bought her beautiful new shoes to make her happy,' says Marina, 'He would put them on her feet. She said, "why are you spending money on that? I can't even stand up."' Nonetheless, the persistence and the exercises began to pay off. She was able to stand, and then take small steps, and eventually begin the process of learning how to walk again.

As soon as she had been able to start walking again, Lubow was back on the bike. First indoors, on the rollers, in small doses. Then building up to gentle loops on the track. The good leg helping the bad one, the cranks doing their work, guiding the foot round. Then building up speed, letting the track do its work too, with its centrifugal slingshot, like when a parent pushes you up on the swing. She watched the other girls race and the itch was there to return. Not in the sprint: that was over. But the pursuit: the purity and simplicity of it. Just you and your rival out there on the other side, playing cat and mouse. The ultimate test of focus and power.

Her doctor wouldn't hear of it. He told her if she raced again she would die. To which Lubow had only one answer; 'everybody's going to die one day.' She persisted, and won the 1955 national championships. She had looked death in the face and come back. It was her speciality.

And now she's catapulting out into the velvety night and the crowd is showering her with oxygen. She is burning in their roar. She is sprinting and there are still 3,000m to go. This cannot last. It is impossible to maintain. Bail knows it. Lubow knows it too, but there is nothing else she can do. It's her only option. Bail is noticeably behind, but she is sensible and pragmatic. She will settle into her powerful rhythm and wait for Lubow to burn out, then move in for the kill.

Lubow must concentrate. There is pain and then there is will. She is burning. She must remember to breathe. To take what her audience is giving her. They are giving her love. She must take it and fuel this terrible fire that threatens to destroy her. Lubow will endure. She has no choice. She is Russian. That's what Russians do.

There is no choice. The KGB man is keeping an eye on them all. De Gaulle has given her a fur coat and invited her to a reception. The whole delegation has to come with her. She says: 'I'm sorry I don't belong to myself. My time doesn't belong to me. I can't make my own decisions.' The prince of Monaco keeps sending her flowers. The KGB man is not happy. 'What do you want from me?' she asks exasperatedly. 'I have done nothing.'

The world championships began with a vetting procedure for the Russians, many months before departure, at which riders lost any privacy they might have had before. They were being observed. They had to weigh every word. You had to avoid being on your own with rivals, in case they put words into your mouth for which you had no witnesses. 'You were even told what clothes to pack in your suitcase', says Marina. And the rules regarding foreigners; 'You could be punished if you said "hello."' Not that that was possible anyway: 'The Soviet Union was a huge country and it was closed. Nobody spoke other languages.'

> De Gaulle has given her a fur coat and invited her to a reception.

If you wanted to go shopping, 'You had to ask the delegation and tell them precisely which store you would visit and at what time.' For the riders, 'it was like going to a museum. They couldn't bring more than $10 out of Russia with them, so they couldn't buy anything anyway.'

They couldn't choose their roommates, either. They always assumed their rooms were bugged. They were used to it, to never being able to openly speak their minds. Lubow and Valentina Maksimova developed a spoken code. Sometimes they would scribble things down on paper, trying to talk naturally all the while, because for someone listening in, 'if you were silent, that was also suspicious'. Everyone complied. 'Soviet people were so afraid. They remembered Stalin's time when people were sent to Siberia without explanations.' Lubow would never have defected, she believed in Communism, despite the paranoia and suspicion, 'It's like you put a bit of poison in a big barrel of honey. It will touch many generations ahead – everything is affected.' But there were also many advantages to being an athlete in the Russian system. 'In the Soviet Union everything was free; you didn't have to pay to use the track, you didn't have to pay for kit and coaches. You didn't have to pay for food or hotels. The physio and massage was free.' They enjoyed another privilege female riders in the West could only dream of: elite riders didn't have to take on other jobs to pay the rent, they could devote all their time to training. While they officially had jobs they were always on 'sabbatical'. On the other hand, if you won a race, you could only receive 5% of your race winnings – the rest went to the state. 'You were like a hero in society, but there were no material gains.' Lubow's fur coat was confiscated by Russian border agents. She used to say, 'If I'd ridden in the West I could have been a multimillionaire.'

And for all the amenities and support elite athletes received during their careers, there was no support or special pensions after they retired, no honorary jobs with special privileges, no matter how many medals you won. Most people had to find work themselves, and this was an obligation, and there was a range of salaries, even in 'normal' life. If you went to university, you would get a better job than if you scraped through school barely getting minimum grades.

The bell rings for the final lap. Bail is coming back. Lubow has given everything she has, but she has to give more. She only has eyes for the track, for the thin black line as it spools and spools. Into the bend and flying out again. Hold the line, hold the line, hold the line. The white noise, the white heat of the crowd. Don't think about anything. Back into the slingshot and now every single thing must count. The line. Silence. The roar. The coach running towards her. They are catching her now.

Marina still has her mother's world champion's medal. It's made of solid gold. She says the Russian team's participation was only confirmed at the last minute, and so while all the other countries are represented on the backs of the winner's medals, the Russian flag is missing. A telegram from Moscow. 'If you are the same Lubow who I treated, I'm very sorry', writes the doctor. 'I have no right to be called a professor. I made the worst mistake of my professional life.' A document worth as much as any medal. She would show it to Marina and say, 'You see! Never trust what the doctors say.'

In Russia Lubow became a household name. 'People couldn't believe that she won, that she had survived the Leningrad hunger and her head injury, and yet won the world championships', explains Marina. Life became an endless round of interviews and invitations to TV chat shows. A distraction, but she didn't have any choice: it was part of what was expected, like being a member of the party.

Six days' training, one day off. The morning on the road and the afternoon on the track. And the cross training: skiing in winter, running and long jump and high jump in the summer. Winter in Tbilisi where you'd meet your friends from the other clubs. If you're lucky you stay in the same hotel. More national championships. More world championships, but this time only bad luck. Punctures at the wrong moment. Another daunting British rider called Beryl Burton. How do you beat that one?

In 1964 Lubow was at a training camp and it was her friend Valentina Maksimova's turn to crash. Lubow ran out to help her. She knew Valentina had an aversion to people touching her, but that she trusted Lubow since they were such close friends. So she tried to drag her off the track. But Valentina was heavy: so much muscle. A three-time world vice champion. If Ermolaeva hadn't been Leonid Brezhnev's favourite rider, and Maksimova hadn't always been instructed to come second, she might have been a gold medallist too.

As Lubow hauled her friend to the track centre she immediately felt something was terribly wrong with her own body. In hospital she learnt she was three months' pregnant. 'She was training so much at that time that she didn't have periods, so she didn't even realize she was pregnant', Marina says. The foetus had little chance of survival, however, and the doctors wanted to abort. Lubow refused. To keep the baby, she had to spend the rest of the pregnancy on her back. She couldn't even lie on her side. On no account could she get out of bed, not even to go to the toilet. So for the next four months she did as she was told, and Marina was eventually born by caesarean, two months premature.

Once again, Lubow had to learn how to walk. It was the end of her athletic career, but she became a coach instead.

Marina grew up on the track – her mother took her everywhere, and she got to know all the riders. Many of them didn't marry or have children, and she became a mascot for them. Tamara Garkushina, the up-and-coming pursuit star, would play with Marina before a final as a way to break the tension. 'I was a tiny creature with a pony tail and they would all play with it. I loved the attention. I didn't realise that they were all stars, that people wanted their autographs. I took it for granted. For me they were just normal people.' As Marina got older her parents' coaching careers meant they were constantly travelling. Both parents were national coaches and as a result had to go to all the races. 'I remember in one calendar year my father was home only 20 days.' Marina would live with her grandmother, but when her mother was back in Tula she wanted to spend every possible moment with her and would accompany her everywhere.

She remembers Lubow being followed by fans down the street and wishing they'd all just go away and leave her mother to herself.

Lubow had many other commitments in addition to coaching. She was made head of a society of people who had survived the Leningrad Blockade. She was a communist deputy entailing endless meetings at the city hall.

Lubow constantly struggled with her health. As a result of her head injuries she would frequently suffer from debilitating headaches. 'She couldn't move or talk, she would be staring into space', Marina recalls. They might occur once a month, or three days in a row and became more frequent as she got older. She got cancer, twice, and suffered a stroke which paralysed her right-hand side. In 2008 the cancer came back a third time. She was given six months but eked out two years.

She never left Tula or its velodrome. 'She was in love with this track. She would ask her friends to take her there and she'd touch it and pat it. She talked to it, like people in church talk to an icon.' Lubow Kotchetova died on 3 November 2010. Evgeniy died a week later. In the Russian Orthodox tradition the body is buried on the third day. But Lubow died just before a national holiday and all the official offices were closed. Marina was able to get the necessary permits for her burial, but couldn't publish any funeral notices. Another Russian tradition is to hold a wake, which, if the person was famous, is held in a setting related to his or her career. In her final days Lubow asked to lie at the Tula velodrome. Marina sat with her mother in the foyer, expecting only a few friends and family members to come.

> 'She was in love with this track. She would ask her friends to take her there and she'd touch it and pat it.'

In the course of the next few hours, thousands of people arrived. 'People were coming and coming. I didn't even know who they were. There were simply fans, people from Tula who loved her, to whom she meant something. Somehow word had got around and they came to say goodbye.'

'The Lone Ranger'

In 1969 Audrey McElmury became the first American, male or female, to win a world championship gold medal in the road race. Her victory had been so unexpected, she'd had to wait on the podium for half an hour in the pouring rain while the organisers tried to find a recording of the US national anthem. More remarkably, her victory took place in the Czech city of Brno, exactly one year after the USSR had sent its tanks in to crush the 'Prague Spring'. There had been rioting the night before, the route of the road race was torn up by tank treads, it rained throughout, and McElmury crashed on the final lap – yet she still won, more than a minute ahead of British rider Bernadette Swinnerton, with a Russian rider, Nina Trofimova, leading the sprint for third place.

In Cold War sports politics, it was a gift for the Americans. Not that they seemed to care or notice. On her return to the US McElmury was greeted by one local TV crew who were more interested in talking about the Russian military occupation than discussing her victory.

If anyone really appreciated McElmury's victory, it was the Czechoslovaks. Just 12 months previously the Russians had not only taken away their reforming leader, Alexander Dubček, and installed a puppet government, but they had done it in the most creepy way possible, entering the country in the dead of night while everyone slept. 'Socialism with a human face' was over: they had taken hope and crushed it underfoot. When a young university student called Jan Palach set himself on fire in Wenceslas Square in January 1969, it was not simply in protest at the Russian occupation, but at the demoralisation of his fellow countrymen. Bernadette Swinnerton (who now goes by her married name, Malvern) was a schoolgirl at the time, studying for her 'A' levels. She vividly remembers the extent of anti-Russian feeling in the Brno velodrome, where Russian riders were greeted, 'with deafening, shrieking whistles during their racing,' while 'every other nationality would be cheered.' When officials threatened to evacuate the spectators if the taunts continued, they adopted another stance: total silence.

When Bernadette lost the quarter-final sprint against the Russian national champion, 'the cheering from 10,000 people followed me round the stadium, whereas absolute silence followed the Russian just a few metres ahead.' When the Russians won the men's team pursuit final, 'The crowd went silent and then immediately emptied out of the stadium in about five minutes, unwilling to watch the medal ceremony and acknowledge Russian superiority.'

Bernadette recalls that there was no racing on the anniversary of the Russian invasion itself, and that riders were warned to stay inside. 'When we ventured out on the 22nd the remains of the previous day's tear gas stung our eyes. The riots had been dreadful. Barricades were still up and there were smashed windows all around. There was soldier presence on every corner. It was said that 5 people had died.'

This, of all days, was the day for the women's road race. The race featured five laps of a hilly 14km circuit featuring a difficult climb with hairpins and a 10% gradient in places. 'Everywhere we rode the roads were a mess', Bernadette recalls. 'There were tanks bordering the road circuit, ready to stop any trouble. The road race organisers attempted to get the surfaces swept on the race circuit, but there just was not enough time before the Ladies' Road Race started. It looked so bad that I decided to race on my training wheels with heavy tyres to ensure I did not puncture.'

Most people assumed the Russians with their six-woman team would dominate the race, as they had almost every year since the women's world championships began in 1958.

Other race favourites were a seven-strong team of Italians and six Dutch riders who included Keetie Hage, the defending champion. Almost immediately, the difficult terrain claimed its first victims, with riders crashing, puncturing and unable to hold the pace on the steep climbs. Bernadette was delighted. 'There was not a single flat stretch and the part I loved most was the two mile long mountain where I stayed either near or on the front each of the five times up.'

For once, here was a race that offered an opportunity to 'sort the wheat from the chaff', as she put it, rather than the usual flat procession towards a sprint that was the norm in women's races. By the start of the climb on the fourth lap there were only 15 riders left.

Audrey McElmury, coming from San Diego, was not used to the rain, but she was good on hills. She was also confident: shortly before coming to Europe she had set a new American women's hour record, riding 24.8 miles (39.912km). And she was ready: in between her part-time job as a lab technician at UCSD (The University of California San Diego) and looking after her baby son, she managed to train twice a day, on the bike and in the gym where she could squat well above her own weight. She ran up and down hundreds of steps, often with a backpack and ankle weights. She was obsessed with good nutrition. After meeting Jacques Anquetil on a previous trip to Europe, she incorporated motor pacing and plenty of intervals into her training. She also raced with men, often coming in the top ten against the best riders in Southern California. She was not a sprinter, however, and if she wanted to win, she had to get away from the peloton. So on the fourth and second to last lap, she attacked on the main climb and opened a 15-second gap.

Audrey did strength training five days a week. © George Coates

Malvern was also in peak condition. 'I had worked hard all year on my climbing ability and was either on the front, or nearly so, every time up the mountain. I chased every single attack until McElmury went. At that point I needed someone else to chase and expected one of the others in the group to take over but no one came through and McElmury got away.' McElmury reached the top of the climb alone and then started the sinuous descent through the trees. Coming into a corner, she started to brake, and her smooth racing tyres slid out from beneath her. 'The pack caught me as I got up', she later wrote. 'The rain was chilly enough that I didn't feel the full effect of my bruised hip, and the rain exaggerated the amount of blood from a cut on my elbows. I chased the pack with an ambulance following me to see if I was all right.' Flushed with adrenalin now, McElmury managed to get back the front group and on the final climb she attacked again.

'My legs were still feeling the result of all my chasing', Malvern recalls, 'but I was certain someone would chase her as they now knew she was a serious threat. I thought to myself, "Let someone else chase, at least she's an English speaker". If she had been a different nationality I *thought* I might have found the strength. My mistake!'

McElmury continued to pull away, in torrential rain. This time coming into the treacherous curve at the bottom of the descent she managed to stay upright, continuing to open her lead. Reaching the bedraggled reporters and scattering of spectators at the finish line she had 40 seconds over the peloton. Bernadette prevailed in the sprint for second place, sailing away from the Russians with a gap of five bike lengths.

McElmury had achieved her life's ambition, to which she had directed so many years' training, for which she'd begged so many hours' childcare and made huge financial sacrifices.

The race was also one of the highlights of Malvern's brief career, but was filled with mixed emotions. 'I was so angry with myself for letting the American get away when the sprint turned out to be so easy for me at the end. For many years, I saw it as a failure. The fact that I was only 18 and had hardly any race experience compared to everyone else, just didn't register.'

On the podium, McElmury put her arm around Trofimova's shoulder, one athlete congratulating another, regardless of nationality or politics. But the loss of the race must have been galling for the Russians, not only because an American won while one of their riders got relegated to third place, but because just about everything about the winner was anathema to their values. McElmury, with her privileged background, had trained to fulfil her own ambitions, she had paid her own way, and she had most certainly ridden for herself – her teammates hadn't even been able to keep up. If her medal brought glory to the US, that was an added bonus, but it was not the reason she rode.

McElmury grew up in the wealthy San Diego suburb of La Jolla, surrounded by high achievers. Her father, Fred B. Phleger, had risen from relatively humble beginnings to become a renowned marine zoologist and palaeontologist at the University of San Diego. Her mother, Marjorie Temple Phleger, was a writer, newspaper columnist and PR executive who was also deeply involved in theatre. Audrey's older brother, Rick Phleger, would become a professor of Biology. In their spare time, both parents wrote children's books, which became popular classics. In one of them, *Anne Can Fly*, a girl with a remarkable resemblance to Audrey learns to fly her father's plane. Theodor Geisel, better known as the children's author Dr Seuss, was a family friend. Another friend, the radiantly beautiful Roberta 'Bobbi' Gibb, would become the first woman to (unofficially) run the Boston marathon in 1966.

At university Audrey was the sort of girl who'd take an advanced mathematics class, 'just for fun'. When she was recovering from a broken leg, her then boyfriend, Scott McElmury, and his brother, Peter, got into cycling. They bought a tandem, and as soon as Audrey was mobile again, she would ride into college on it with Scott to rebuild her strength.

Together with Scott and Peter she joined the American Youth Hostels bicycling programme, which operated as a cycling club, and a fancy one at that, offering a busy programme of rides, picnics, camping trips and courses in 'leadership'. As one of its newsletters put it; 'Do you ever stop to realize that you belong to the best organized, best equipped bicycle club in America? A club with all the trimmings: trailers, rollers, clubroom, bicycle shop, hostel, bus, camping equipment, old-fashioned high wheels, unicycles, everything. A club with the know-how to organize bicycle vacations under capable leaders, both here and abroad. A club with some of the finest people you will ever meet anywhere.'

Working the rainbow jersey look in the California sun.
© Audrey Elmury Collection

In 1963, the programme's founder, Dr Clifford Graves, organised a 10-week cycling tour of Europe which Audrey, Scott and Peter took part in. Graves made sure all his young acolytes ordered a René Herse frame for the trip. Each rider had to contribute $800 for the trip and $200 for clothes, bike and camera, about $8,000 dollars in total in today's money.

At the end of their tour they visited the René Herse shop. A photographer from *Le Figaro* wanted to photograph the Americans in front of the Arc de Triomphe and so Lyli, the reigning French national champion and René's daughter, jumped on her bike and told them to follow her.'

'Even though she was probably taking it easy, the pace was fast,' Scott later recalled. 'Fighting to stay on her wheel was all fun as we flew along the back streets of Paris. Getting dropped here meant not being in the picture, as several of the group found out.' The trip triggered a life-long love of Europe and a passion for cycling. On their return to the US, Audrey and Scott got married, and they also joined the San Diego Bicycle Club where their training became more serious. They began racing and Audrey quickly excelled in local events.

In the US in 1963, the women's racing scene was almost non-existent. There was a women's national championship, but only on the track. Audrey became a very good pursuit rider, but she preferred to be out on the road, and so began to ride in men's races.

When the first national road race for women was finally introduced in 1966, her training with more aggressive riders paid off. Despite crashing in the first mile and chasing two riders for 20 miles until just before the finish, McElmury won. She also took the national pursuit title. In the same year she set US records in the 3,000m and the 25 mile time trial.

When she became pregnant at the end of the year she continued to train and race, riding 4,000 miles in the course of her pregnancy. Two days before giving birth she was doing squats with a 135 pound barbell.

McElmury's win in Brno hadn't come out of nowhere. But afterwards, the effort that had gone into achieving it began to take its toll. The following season McElmury appeared to sink into a depression. She won her national road race and pursuit championships but started skipping races and training sessions. Her relationship with her husband began to deteriorate. Perhaps, being an ambitious rider himself, he'd been jealous of her success, or her devotion to her 4.30am training rides. Perhaps she felt suffocated by the demands of work, child rearing, maintaining her homelife and training. When she went to the 1971 worlds in Italy, she dragged her heels coming back, and ended up travelling round Europe for a few weeks with another rider she'd met, a New Yorker called Michael Levonas. She returned to the US, but only briefly. A crisis of some sort sent her flying back to Europe, where she moved into a flat with Levonas in Southern Spain. Around the same time a new, commercially sponsored, Italian women's team expressed interest in hiring her for the following season. She reached a crisis point: should she go back to her family and fulfil the role expected of her as a wife and mother, or stay in Europe and live the dream of riding for a sponsored women's team?

A friend and training partner, Armin Janzen, sympathised with her dilemma: 'I can visualize what contortions your mind must be going through when it comes to decisions of coming home or the bike', he wrote. 'We both have something that drives us inside to ride that fucking machine at any cost and it just works out that a man's one-sidedness is accepted more readily.'

McElmury returned to the US, where she had to deal with a messy divorce and began adjusting to a new life as a single mother. Yet to everyone's surprise, perhaps including her own, she was back with Levonas in Europe in April, with her son, and a full time job as a racing cyclist. The 'pay' consisted of board, lodging, childcare and anything she won in races. The team was sponsored by CBM, a family-run factory specialising in car parts. The Italians lived up to every cliché. When McElmury won a hill climb, she later recalled, 'everyone kissed me and it was like a drunken brawl afterwards.' Before a race, 'Everyone would go to bed very late and very full of wine. That was due to our so-called "pre-race meeting."' The morning of a race would start in a panic at 8am with chaos and shouting, even if the race wasn't taking place until the afternoon and was only an hour's drive away. At one point the team forgot to strap another rider's bike onto the team car, and it fell off down a ravine.

There were plenty of prizes to be won, some odder than others. Audrey would come back with things like a brace of pheasants, a fur hat, a toaster, stockings, an iron, perfume, cake, vases, vitamins,

an ashtray, a belt, bottles of wine, a book, suitcases, a framed picture or a set of pans.

On one occasion she crashed and was taken to hospital for stitches. The race organisers waited for her return before handing out the prizes. McElmury received a 'bad luck' prize in the form of a comfy armchair. Her teammate Jana, she recounted, 'won a huge grandfather's clock, which she managed to tie on top of her Fiat 500 for the ride home. Others won tables, couches, chairs, lamps, etc. We looked like a gypsy caravan or a Good Will excursion leaving the parking lot, with various pieces of the furniture and bicycles strapped on our vehicle.' McElmury would later consider her year in Italy one of the happiest of her life.

Her last great achievement as a cyclist was to break her own US 25-mile time trial record, with a time of 1.00:315 in June 1974. McElmury's life was more complex of course than any Cold War symbolism would allow. If she enjoyed the relative freedoms of life in a capitalist system, she also experienced its dark side. Choosing the bike over a normal career, she constantly struggled for money. Competing in a sport that was undervalued and ignored in the US, her achievements went largely under the radar. By the time other great American female riders started to emerge, McElmury was largely forgotten. Her first husband, Scott, later wrote:

'On numerous occasions over the past 25 years, while sitting around with other bike riders, I would casually mention that my first wife was World Road Champion in 1969. The reaction is usually the same. First a brief silence then questions of the type:
"There were American women racing bicycles in the '60s?"
"There was a woman's road world championship in 1969?"
"How many women in the race – ten or fifteen?"
"How could an American have won – did all the European women fall down?"
I never have the time or energy to fully explain what she accomplished and that it was definitely not a fluke, particularly the manner in which she won. I always go away feeling frustrated that the present day cycling community knows little or nothing about Audrey McElmury, 1969 World Road Champion.'

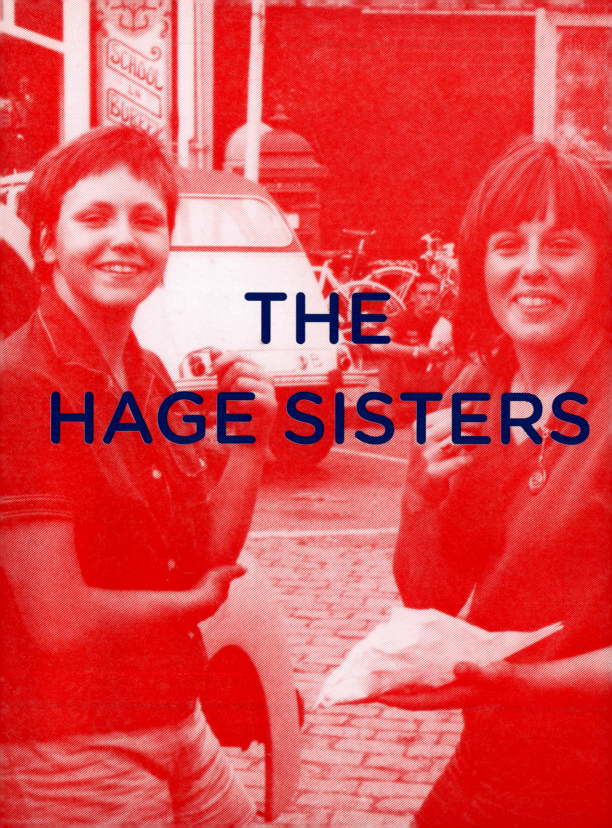

'The flying Dutch women'

There was a time when the whole of the Dutch women's peloton pitted itself against two or three riders. They were sisters: Bella, Keetie, Ciska and Heleen Hage. Bella was the pioneer, Keetie was the 'cannibal' who won everything, Ciska raced only briefly before moving onto other things and Heleen, born ten years after Bella, won three stages and came second overall in the inaugural women's Tour de France.

Between Keetie and Bella, no other Dutch rider came close to winning the Dutch national championships between 1966 and 1976. A whole generation of riders developed race strategies with the sole ambition of beating the sisters. And mostly, they failed. 'We were sometimes rivals, but always the most important thing was that *one* of us won, so we worked together too', Bella recalls. 'One year we tried to get all three of us on the podium, Keetie, Heleen and me. Unfortunately Heleen broke her collarbone about a week before the race, otherwise I think we could have done it.' When they weren't swapping the national championship title between each other, they would represent Holland at the world championships, where Keetie won a staggering 19 medals including six gold – two on the road and four on the track. With Bella and Heleen's support, Keetie also twice conquered the Red Zinger (later named the Coors Classic), an eight-day stage race in Colorado which was the biggest women's stage race in the world at the time, both in terms of scope and prize money. And when she wasn't winning races, Keetie also broke the women's hour record, just for the hell of it.

In the Hage family everyone raced; four girls and two boys. Their father simply loved riding his bike, and passed that enthusiasm onto his children.

Anthonie 'Toon' Hage was the fifth generation of a farming family from the island of Tholen in the windswept province of Zeeland. Farming might have been his destiny, but it wasn't Toon's cup of tea. His great passion on Sundays was to get on his bike, and he joined a club in Roosendaal, a town 40km away. From the time his first and second children, Bella and Keetie, were about 12 and 11 respectively, he would bring them on his rides as well.

'We'd cycle 40km to Roosendaal, then ride with the club for about 40-50km, then ride the 40km back', Bella recalls. Sometimes they would join a ride setting out from Antwerp, 60km away. So they'd ride there, do a 60km club ride, then cycle home again. By this point the two sisters were still only 13 or 14 years old.

Bella and Keetie live about 40km from each other now in neat, modern homes. Bella's has a shed filled with her and her husband's many bikes. On Keetie's dining room wall hang a series of hand-painted Delft plates – mementoes of some of her great victories. They still enjoy getting on their bikes. Bella goes on touring holidays with her husband. One summer they spent three months riding from coast to coast across the USA.

Touring holidays are not Keetie's idea of fun. She takes her young grandchildren out on 25km rides and does 50-70km on her racing bike twice a week. Every spring she likes to ride up the Mont Ventoux. There's an 86km bike circuit around Tholen named in her honour. Her grandchildren will no doubt grow up thinking it's entirely normal to see their granny's name signposted everywhere, alongside a symbol of a bike and windsock.

Bella started racing in 1965 when she was not quite 17. That same year the Dutch cycling federation ran its first ever national championship road race for women, where Bella came second. The following year she took her first of three consecutive victories. After that Keetie took over. 'I was not so lucky having Keetie as my sister', Bella says drily.

When she started out, Bella had no idea about racing. 'I had no idea what gears to use!' she laughs. Her father was similarly clueless, and, 'not such a good mechanic', either. He was, however, the girls' biggest fan, and would spend every weekend taking them to races. They would crisscross Holland, but also go to Belgium, France and even Italy in his Volkswagen Beetle with the bikes on a rack. As for tactical race advice, 'He would tell us, "just do your best."' Keetie recalls.

Bella vividly remembers her first race in Belgium when she was 17. It featured 70 one-km laps of an entirely cobbled circuit around the Vogeltjesmarkt in Antwerp. It was an evening race and Bella had already ridden 40km that day as part of her commute to work. She remembers it as one of her worst race experiences ever. The Belgians were merciless, with more than ten years' racing experience in their legs and two world champions, Yvonne Reynders and Marie-Rose Gaillard, in their arsenal. 'They started so fast, I went straight to the back of the peloton', she recalls. She was behind the field when Gaillard lapped everyone and Bella managed to latch onto her wheel. 'I had no idea who she was or what place she was. I just latched on. Everyone was shouting.' Bella nearly made it back to the bunch when Gaillard was about to lap the field again, but couldn't hold on. The judges pulled her out a few laps before the end of the race. It never crossed her mind to abandon; 'we had no idea what it was, not to finish.'

'The next day at work they said, what did you *do* yesterday evening? My hands were all open and bleeding from the vibrations from the cobbles.' It took her a while to figure things out. 'I had no idea about sprinting. I was always too late at the front. At the last turn you have to be in the first three or four at least.' The Belgian races might have been infernal, but they offered a masterclass in an aggressive style of racing which would become Keetie's hallmark in particular.

In Holland it was a different scene altogether. The Dutch races were only 20 or 30km long, child's play to what was on offer in Belgium. The Belgians would cross the border and take home all the prizes. But it didn't take long for the Hage sisters to assert themselves. Very rapidly they began winning all the local races themselves, so that race organisers were obliged to increase distances in the misguided belief this would give their rivals more of a chance.

The prizes themselves weren't much to write home about. 'One year I won four irons', recalls Bella. Another year, Keetie won five. Later on, when cash prizes became more commonplace, you might get 25 guilders, Bella says, with which you could 'maybe buy a cheap pair of shoes'. With the 2.5 guilders you got if you came tenth, you might splash out on a couple of coffees.

Bella was eventually eclipsed by Keetie, who surprised everyone by winning the world championships in 1968 when she was only 19 years old. The next year she won the first of her 9 national championships, 8 of them consecutive.

Right from the off, it was clear that Keetie had an outstanding talent. Unlike Bella, she came second in her first race in Belgium. 'None of the Dutch girls could keep up with the peloton, but I was in the breakaway with Marie-Rose Gaillard', she recalls. Marie-Rose and Keetie worked together to stay away and the Belgian prevailed on the finish line. 'At that point I knew I was good', says Keetie with a giggle – which is about as close as she will ever get to boasting.

> Keetie says she loved racing – 'it got me off the island and allowed me to see the world.'

Both sisters are astonishingly modest – as much a reflection of their characters as the Old Reform Church culture that pervades the province of Zeeland. But the villagers of St Maartensdijk certainly enjoyed a party and they would celebrate every time the sisters won a major race. They formed a supporters club and would hire two buses every year so they could cheer the girls at the national championships. They helped financially, too, one year clubbing together to buy Keetie a lighter racing frame.

Keetie says she loved racing – 'it got me off the island and allowed me to see the world.' In the late 1970s, towards the end of their careers, the sisters were invited to the women's edition of the Red Zinger, a stage race in Boulder, Colorado, where they rode against the queen of American cycling, Connie

Carpenter. Carpenter had so few American rivals that the race organiser decided to invite some Europeans. The Dutch brought a little too much competition for Carpenter's tastes, however, and Keetie became her sworn enemy. 'She was feisty, tough and relentless on the bike, and very quiet off the bike', Connie would write later. 'Whenever she won (which was often) she would throw up her hands in a manner that suggested she had never won before. She'd celebrate with her hands to the sky and her face was lit up like a Christmas tree. I have to admit, it drove me crazy. I really wanted to beat her. If you have ever pushed yourself on the bike to a very high level and had someone take off and attack you from that level – well, that was Keetie. She could break my chops just about any day of the week.' Keetie won the race two years running. The first year she won the opening time trial with more than a minute over Connie, then held the lead for the duration of the race. Another time she prevailed in a criterium stage held in a downpour. There were generous *primes* worth, 'more than a 100 dollars!' Keetie recalls. Connie crashed several times on the slick roads, as did most of the rest of the field. Keetie, with her race smarts honed in Belgium, weaved her way through the carnage. She did all this despite being jetlagged by 8 hours; since she and her teammates had to take holiday leave from work in order to compete, they would arrive the day before the race began.

> 'She was feisty, tough and relentless on the bike, and very quiet off the bike.'

Keetie also excelled on the track, winning four gold medals in the pursuit at the world championships and 12 consecutive national titles. But it wasn't really her thing: she found racing in velodromes 'boring', she confesses, 'and also it was a two hours' drive to Amsterdam just to train.' At the Amsterdam velodrome there was no shortage of male riders suggesting she take up ballet or gymnastics instead. Racing, they said, wasn't for girls.

Bella says Keetie was a much more determined rider. In the end, Bella was more interested in riding just for pleasure. Keetie says Bella had a better sprint, especially after 70km when everyone was flagging. Keetie says she had stamina, and would always be on the attack, even at the start of a race. She didn't trust her chances of prevailing if she left everything to the final sprint. 'There was always Geneviève Gambillon sitting on my wheel', she says. The sisters called her 'the Truck' since Gambillon sounds a bit like the French word *camion*, and no one could get past her when she really let fly. She didn't care too much for Beate Habetz, either, the West German 1978 world champion, 'if I fell back she never did her share. Once we were a long way behind the peloton and she still wouldn't help.'

In the 1976 world championships a mechanic finally gave Keetie the advice and confidence to temper her efforts. 'He said I should attack only once, and if that didn't work, I should just stay in the peloton and fight it out at the finish.' She'd had seven years of being pipped to the post and figured she might as well give it a try. To her great surprise and delight, she found she had what was needed to sail past her rivals at the end, to win a second road race gold medal.

Two years later another mechanic suggested she have a go at the hour. She had just won the 1978 world championship pursuit in Munich and she liked the track there. So they waited for the right conditions. Finally, on a Friday evening in September, just a few days before the track closed, they got on a plane to Munich. Keetie came straight from teaching at school. The following morning she practised on the track and in the afternoon she broke the hour record. Just like that. Afterwards she would describe it as the hardest hour of her life. She covered a distance of 43.082km – adding 1.611m to the record set by Maria Cressari in 1972. Her record would eventually be broken by Jeannie Longo in 1986.

Then she was back at work on Monday, as if nothing had happened. She never told her students about her double identity. Sometimes she would get children coming up to her saying, 'my mum told me you were world champion'. 'And after that, I'd get children saying, "my granny says you were world champion". That's how you know you're getting old!' she laughs.

Keetie's memorabilia is neatly pasted into books, together with extensive cuttings, although she says she never looks at them. At one point she fishes out a couple of rainbow jerseys. Most of them she gave away. One is a bit yellowed, from having spent some years on the wall of a pub.

I ask her if she found it hard to retire. 'I didn't have the "black hole" after I stopped racing because I had my children straight after I stopped, and then I had my work as a teacher', she tells me. 'Riders now, they don't have that – their whole lives have been about cycling, and when they retire they have nothing. Life is about more than racing.'

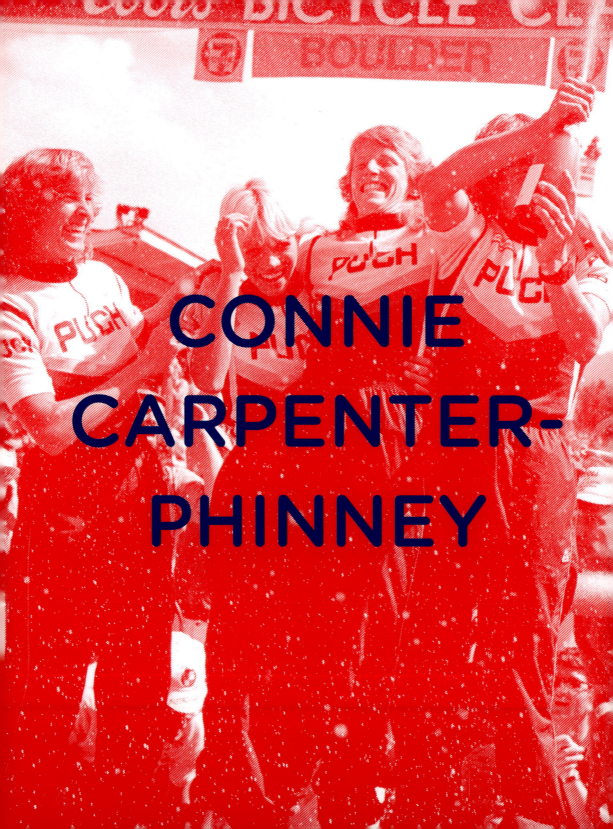

CONNIE CARPENTER-PHINNEY

'The Ice Queen'

The Americans were late coming to cycling, and when they eventually did, it was the women who led the way, first with Audrey McElmury, the first American to win a world championship road race, in 1969, then with Marianne Martin, the first American to win the Tour de France, in 1984, and finally with Connie Carpenter-Phinney, the first American to win an Olympic road race, one week after Martin's triumph.

In McElmury's case, it took 14 years for a man to catch up. In Martin's case, it took two years (in both instances it was Greg LeMond who ended the drought). In Carpenter-Phinney's case, it took only a few hours. The man who followed her, however, was not her husband, Davis Phinney, as all the pundits had predicted, but his teammate, Alexi Grewal. So Connie's greatest moment of athletic triumph happened to fall on the same day as her husband's most bitter disappointment.

Connie was the golden girl of American cycling, the ultimate Alpha athlete. With her delicate, angular features and strawberry blonde hair, she was also an instantly recognisable icon, an ice-cool, fine-boned Valkyrie.

Long before she became a cyclist, she had been a precociously talented speed skater who was only 14 when she took part in her first Olympics in Japan in 1972. Connie learned to skate in the long, cold winters in Wisconsin where she grew up. She lived across the street from a school playground that was flooded in winter so that it froze and became an ice-skating rink. Every evening the lights went on between 7 and 9pm, and Connie, her three brothers and the rest of the children in the village would all spend hours playing on the ice. 'If you have never skated under lights on a dark night, you may not know the acute sensation of speed that accompanies the lessening of peripheral vision that darkness brings,' she later wrote. 'The skills I learned allowed me to be elusive when chased – and effective when I was the chaser. That gave me a sense of power beyond my age.'

Connie won every junior local speed skating championship from kindergarten through to sixth grade (around the age of 11). Every year the local speed skating club would ask her to join their team, and every year her parents would turn the invitation down: there was enough to do looking after her older brothers and their hockey lives.

When, eventually, her parents were persuaded to fit Connie's desires into their already hectic family programme, it marked a turning point for their daughter. 'Sport gave me an instant sense of community and a purpose that had structure,' she wrote. It also provided an escape from social pressure at school. 'I could be one person in school (a rather mysterious, good student) and another person across town (athlete and a good one at that).' Connie was selected for the Olympic team in 1972. At the Olympics in Sapporo, Japan, she witnessed two of her teammates — Anne Henning and Dianne Holum — win gold medals, while Connie herself came 7th in the 1,500m race.

Another skater on the team was Sheila Young, who was also a track cyclist, who in 1973 became the first non-Russian in 15 years to win gold in the sprint at the world championships. Connie started cross training with Sheila on the track but it wasn't until an ankle injury ruined her chances of making the 1976 Olympic team, however, that she took up road cycling instead. Straight away in her first season that same year she won the national championship road race and the 3,000m pursuit on the track.

Back at college in Wisconsin, Connie would race in men's and women's races. The women's races were invariably short – between 5 and 15 miles at the most – and the men's were usually held a few hours later. Riding and racing against men became a crucial element to her training throughout her cycling career, forcing her to up her game. Once a week her club would race on the roads of an abandoned military base outside Madison. 'Those races honed my cornering and breakaway skills – and put me right where I needed training-wise – on the rivet.' By 1977 she had become the top female cyclist in America, winning the national championships in both the road race and the 3,000m pursuit, the Fitchburg Longsjo Classic and the general classification of the Coors Classic women's stage race out in Colorado. She also won a silver medal at the world championships in Venezuela.

In contrast to the 'secretive' culture of speed skaters, who trained alone, Connie revelled in the 'festival-like atmosphere', of cycling. She took a break from her studies and moved with her then boyfriend, who also raced at the top level, to Berkeley, California – another college town with a strong cycling culture, where they lived the 'counter-culture vagabond cycling life', living in a bedsit with a mattress on the floor, surviving off very little and training and racing constantly.

Connie was unbeatable on home turf, but then the Coors Classic brought in some foreign riders, including the Dutch rider Keetie Hage and her sister Heleen. Keetie dominated the race, much to Carpenter's fury. Connie even spent a few weeks racing in Holland to get her revenge, 'chasing, attacking and taking advantage of the local peloton politics to break away and win a few on my own.

She had thrown the gauntlet down in my home turf, it was the least I could do to return the favour.'

In 1979 Connie won the national championships for the third time in both the road race and pursuit, but a concussion following a bad crash that year, together with a growing frustration at the lack of opportunities for women's racing, made Connie put the racing to one side. 'I had nowhere to go – there was no Olympics, no sponsorships – and I had won enough national championships that I didn't care about winning another one.' Back at university, this time at Berkeley, where she was studying physical education, she took up rowing, and within six months was on the varsity team. Her tall, lean body, already fine-tuned to high intensity endurance efforts, offered the perfect raw material for a rower, she just had to learn the technique, which she did fast, just like everything she applied herself to. In 1980 her varsity women's coxed four shell won the national collegiate championship.

> Connie had only one aim in mind: to become the Olympic champion.

During this time she started dating her future husband, Davis Phinney, who was part of the Boulder, Colorado cycling scene and so successful at winning races people called him 'The Cash Register'. While visiting the Coors Classic, Connie realised how much she missed racing. Davis then delivered a blow to her pride by suggesting she hadn't yet lived up to her potential as a cyclist. With the announcement that there would be a women's road race in the 1984 Olympics, it was all she needed to get back into the sport. From 1981 when she graduated until 1984, Connie had only one aim in mind: to become the Olympic champion.

Settling in Boulder she cobbled together a team of like-minded women with similar ambitions. Sponsorship had improved thanks to the glamour of Olympic recognition and she was able to just about scrape by as a full-time cyclist without having to take on a paying job – something most female riders at that point could still only dream about.

A key teammate for Connie was Sue Novara-Reber, a sprint specialist who had twice won the world championships in the sprint on the track. Sue became Connie's guru in all things sprint-related, a rider who was not only very powerful but who had the smarts regarding all those crucial split-second decisions. 'Sue knew how to take advantage of the terrain, her competitors and the bike.'

At one point the women went to France to take part in a series of races, in miserable conditions. They were put up in school dormitories, stuck in buildings with no heating or blankets on the beds and given food that 'lacked any nutritional content'. They piled all their clothes onto their beds to keep warm, yet were still unable to sleep. Then they had to race in the rain. As they gazed

despondently out of the window, Sue said: 'They treat us as women imitating men, not as female athletes. We don't belong here – we are not one of them.'

That was a turning point for Connie. Until then it had been – still is – established wisdom in the US that if you really want to up your game in cycling, you need to go to Europe. That's where you learn your craft, get your baptism of fire competing against riders brought up on mud and cobblestones, where you might catch the eye of a directeur sportif who might open the door to a feeder teem which may or may not give you an entrée into the professional ranks.

Connie realised this simply wasn't true as far as women were concerned. She had everything she needed back home: there was (some) money, there was an excellent women's stage race and, most significantly, no one was stopping her from riding in men's amateur races. For a top female cyclist, there could be no better place to refine your craft.

And there were rivals, too, one of whom, in particular, was threatening to take away Connie's crown.

Rebecca Twigg, from Seattle, was six years younger than Connie. She was so bright, she'd gone to the University of Washington aged 14 to study Biology. Painfully shy, she soon immersed herself in the world of bike racing, at which she proved equally brilliant. Between 1979 and 1984 she won 10 of the 16 national titles of her career, in both junior and senior categories, in every discipline imaginable on both the track and the road. In 1982 the pursuit world championships in Leicester ended in a duel between Connie and Rebecca, and Rebecca won. The following year in Zürich, the roles were reversed. In 1984 Rebecca would prevail again in Barcelona. In total she would win 6 titles in the course of her career.

In 1983 she would win the Coors Classic after Connie crashed out with a broken elbow and she came second in the world championships road race behind the Swedish rider Marianne Berglund. Eddie Borysewicz, the Polish coach the Americans had brought in to coach their national team – in the hope of learning a few Eastern Bloc tricks with which to beat their Soviet rivals – had been straight onto her, and took her under his wing. In the run-up to the Olympics, she was installed at the US Olympic training centre in Colorado Springs.

While Rebecca was being coached in Colorado Springs, Connie was following her own programme for Olympic domination. From the moment she saw the route for the women's race outside LA in January, until the day of the race on Sunday 29 June, she rode 80% of her races against category 1 men. Not only was this efficient, since it meant she spent less time travelling and offered more training opportunities, but it also immersed her in a 'more aggressive style of racing'.

'I resisted the temptation to race the full distance in races that were too long because I wanted to be fast and going the distance was not an issue for me. I focused on faster shorter races that required bike handling and tactics, and forced me to stay at or near my limit for a good portion of the race.' Connie and Davis got married in 1983, and as the hype built for the Olympics, they became the royal couple of US cycling, each of them a safe bet for gold – or at the very least a medal – in their respective races.

But there was the question of Rebecca, too. Now it was confirmed they were both on the team, would they support each other if it came down to it in the race? In an interview with the *Los Angeles Times* the previous year, Connie had made it clear they weren't friends: 'She's made the mistake of saying some things about me in the press.' One thing that's without a doubt is that both women were supremely confident in their abilities. 'At some point in my career I might just have to win every race I'm in just to keep improving,' Rebecca told one paper in 1983. Connie, on the other hand, considered herself the number one contender for the Olympics. 'I have more experience and I want to win more than anybody else', she told the *Los Angeles Times*. 'I'd kill myself to win if it came down to that.'

> 'I'd kill myself to win if it came down to that.'

The women's road race was the opening event of the 1984 Olympics, held in Mission Viejo about 50 miles south of Los Angeles. An estimated 200,000 lined the course, many of whom had 'set up camps the day before and held overnight barbecue parties to keep their places. Some climbed trees for a better view, and a few climbed streetlights. Crowds waved flags and chanted "U!S!A! U!S!A!"' It was hot, and the 79km course was hilly. As the peloton reached the feed zone on the third lap, Twigg broke away, powering up the 12.5% incline of Vista del Lago, which the American riders had nicknamed Suicide Hill. She managed a gap of about 15 seconds before the Italian rider Maria Canins hauled her in. A mountains specialist, no one was getting away from Maria on a mere hill. 'She is so strong she goes out and gets you', Connie later said. On Maria's wheel came a select group, featuring Connie, the 17-year-old Sandra Schumacher, in her third consecutive year as the West German national road race champion, who had won the inaugural *Postgiro* stage race in Norway at the age of only 16, Unni Larsen, a Norwegian and that year's victor of the *Postgiro* who was also a competitive dog-sled racer, and the much-feared Jeannie Longo, whose killer sprint had already won her 6 consecutive national champion's jerseys and that year's Tour of Texas.

Such a formidable group of riders was never going to be caught by the peloton, and for the last two laps they worked together to stay away.

Canins, conscious that she was no match for the others in the sprint, went off first with 500m to go, perhaps hoping to take them all by surprise. Forced to respond, they came out after her, accelerating far too early for their tastes. Longo and Canins converged and suddenly the Italian's pedal ended up in the French riders' wheel, breaking her chain. With 200m to go it was now Schumacher leading the pack, but Twigg was right on her tail. In the last 80m she swung off to Schumacher's left and catapulted herself forward. Connie came up on Schumacher's right, intent on catching Rebecca. Rebecca held her lead, digging deep with all the fire and optimism of her 21 years. But Connie was onto her, gaining in velocity with every fraction of a second. As they hurtled towards the line Rebecca had the edge. In the heat of the afternoon and the noise of the crowd, Connie remained ice cool. She remembered everything her friend Sue Novara-Reber had taught her. And Davis: all the drills and discussions and long-distance phone calls when he was racing in Europe now crystallised in the bright Californian sun. Here she was. This was it. With one final effort she thrust her handlebars forward and threw her bike over the line.

Surrounded by a wall of noise, she threw her arm around Rebecca and kissed her on the cheek. They were ecstatic, not quite sure who'd won, certain only that they held gold and silver between them. Schumacher came in third, Unni Larsen fourth, Canins fifth, a devastated Longo sixth, on foot.

It was a pivotal moment for so many things; for American road racing, for women's road racing, for women's sport in general. These striking, all-American girls, winning America's first gold and silver medals, in front of hundreds of thousands of screaming fans. It was the moment the modern era of women's cycling began.

Connie and Rebecca Twigg celebrate. 1984 Olympics © Peter Read Miller/Sports Illustrated/Getty

1984 Olympic road race. © John W. McDonough/Sports Illustrated/Getty

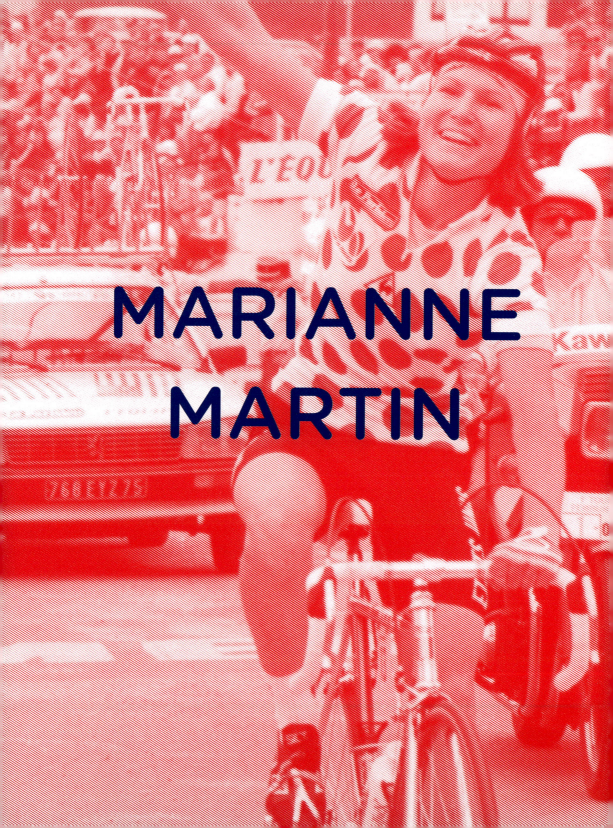

'La Championne'

No one expected Marianne Martin to win the inaugural women's Tour de France. Not her father, who was worrying about when she was going to get herself a proper job. Not her great friend Steve Tilford, who'd been teasing her about the fact that he'd dropped her on some climbs that spring. Not the coach for the American cycling programme, Eddie Borysewicz, who'd given her the last spot on the team, but only after she'd driven two hours to see him, waited two more, and pleaded with him to take her on. Not the sports editors, many of whom didn't even know there was a women's Tour de France. And certainly not Marianne herself, who knew her job was to ride as best as she could to support the team's leader, Betsy King.

After all, she had only been racing for three years, and she was still recovering from a strength-sapping bout of anaemia that she'd had in the spring. 'Have you ever been at altitude?' she asks. 'It's a bit like that feeling where it's hard to get enough air. But as soon as I'd heard the winter before that there was a women's Tour de France, I was like, *that's* what I want to do. I didn't care about the Olympics, I didn't care about anything else. I wanted to do the Tour de France. But even in May I was riding really badly', she recalls. 'So I didn't have any expectations or goals.' 1984 was to be a momentous summer for women's cycling, there would not only be a women's Tour de France, but also the first ever women's cycling event at the Olympics, a 49.2 mile (79.2km) road race. Although given that only a week – and some 9,000km – separated the end of the Tour and the Olympic road race in LA, most of the international federations decided to send their top riders – legendary figures like Jeannie Longo, Maria Canins and Connie Carpenter-Phinney among them – to the Olympics. But for Martin, in the upper echelons of the US women's cycling programme but not quite in the cut for the Olympic team, it was a mystery why anyone would choose the Olympics over the Tour.

'To me, that's the pinnacle! It's celebratory, it's passionate, it's *long*. In a one-day race anything can happen, but a stage race like that really shows who's the champion. To me that was the pinnacle of everything. And it was an adventure, so unknown and everything...'

Martin had grown up in Fenton, Michigan, but had settled in Boulder, Colorado, where she went to university. She fell into cycling while waitressing during the Coors Classic, which at that point held the most ambitious women's stage

race in the world. The whole scene – the racing, and the parties that followed – seemed like so much fun.

She joined a club: 'I just wanted to ride with people and go to the parties', she recalls. 'Then I found out you couldn't do that, you had to race!' It turned out she was a natural who routinely crossed the line first in races involving mountains. But while the racing gave her a thrill, she says primarily, 'I loved riding and I loved riding hard.'

Felix Lévitan, the financial director of the Tour de France, was taking a big gamble by launching a women's race. Just as when Henri Desgrange announced the first ever Tour of 1903, many commentators thought the riders wouldn't make it to the finish. But he himself was adamant it had to happen. The momentum that was building for women's cycling was undeniable. And then there was his wife, who was hassling him about it too.

He knew that women were capable of remarkable feats of strength and endurance: in 1983 Joan Benoit had set a new women's marathon record in Boston with a time of 2:22:43, running faster than the great French Algerian champion Alain Mimoun on the occasion of his 1956 Olympic victory. Lévitan had also witnessed first hand Beryl Burton's remarkable performance against the men at the Grand Prix des Nations in 1968 – indeed he'd been the man who'd given her permission to start. And his wife had been one of the first to congratulate her, presenting her with a giant bouquet.

He knew all about the women's edition of the Coors Classic and he knew very well that it could be done. He also knew the future of cycling was in America. If nothing else, that was where the money was. When Jonathan Boyer became the first American to ride the Tour in 1981, Lévitan could see the sponsors' dollars pouring in, and insisted Boyer ride in a stars and stripes jersey, even though he wasn't the US champion. Greg Lemond meanwhile confirmed American ascendance with his world championship triumph in 1983.

> 'I have absolutely nothing against women's sports, but cycling is much too diffcult for a woman. They are not made for the sport...'

There would be a women's tour, it would be made up of national teams, and one of those would be American. Come what may. Quite a few Frenchmen, however, thought the whole business preposterous, not least Jacques Anquetil, the five-time Tour de France winner, who wrote in *L'Equipe*; 'I have absolutely nothing against women's sports, but cycling is much too difficult for a woman. They are not made for the sport. I am sorry to see women suffer. On a bicycle, there's always a lot of suffering.' The Americans were bemused, but hardly troubled, by such attitudes. Back home they were used to being taken seriously as athletes, and they often trained and raced with men. Only a few months previously, Betsy King had been the first woman to take part in the 600km Bordeaux–Paris race, just to prove it could be done. She'd had a head start of two hours, and finished 10 minutes behind the last man (four others abandoned the race). 'I wanted to show that women could do it, because I think we have better endurance than men, even over longer distances, despite the fact that we're weaker', she said afterwards. It never even occurred to any of the women that they couldn't do it.

'It was so fun, it was so bizarre,' Martin says of her first impressions of the race. 'You know in the States it's very controlled; you have to do *this* and you do *this*... In France it was a little bit – and I say this in a good, loving way – it was a little bit chaotic.'

And so the race began, rolling out of the suburb of Bobigny north east of Paris. There were six national teams, each featuring six amateur riders. Their stages featured the same roads and mountain passes as the men's race, only they would start out two hours earlier and cover shorter distances to comply with UCI regulations. Their race featured 991km (616 miles) in total, over 18 stages, to the men's 4,019km (2,500 miles) and 23 stages.

As the Americans set off, they were under strict instructions from back home to ride for King, a 34-year old from Connecticut who now lived in France and had won so many races there she'd even toyed with the idea of taking French citizenship.

The 'team' might have had a leader, but it didn't have a strategy. There had been no training camp where they could get to know each other before the race. There wasn't even a budget for an American Directeur Sportif, so they got stuck with a Frenchman who didn't speak English. Marianne, however, did have some idea of what needed doing, from all the race wisdom she'd picked up from male training partners who rode on sponsored teams. The problem was, quite a few other women on the team had ideas too, and they weren't the same. There was a lot of infighting. Her first surprise was coming third in the first stage, despite not being a sprinter. 'I was more worried about getting behind a crash, and so I just rode conservatively but strong up front', she explains. That little flourish caused a few problems, however. As a domestique, she wasn't allowed to 'shine', as she puts it, 'so I actually got in trouble'.

After that, Martin kept a low profile, doing her best to be a good teammate while the very organised Dutch team, headed by Keetie and Bella Hage's younger sister Heleen, took the race led.

As the race zig-zagged across the flatter parts of Northern France, the Dutch set to work winning all the stages, routinely taking the top three spots of each day's racing. While they were bitter rivals on the road, however, Martin loved their racing spirit. 'They were fabulous "sportifs,"' she recalls. 'They would always say "congratulations" or "good race."' They were also the perfect example of what could be achieved with a well-organised team, which made Martin doubly conscious of her own, somewhat dysfunctional band.

Everything changed on the 12th stage, which ended in Grenoble and featured two mountain passes, the 2nd category Col du Rousset and the 1st category Col de Chalimont.

By this point in the race Marianne had been thinking about her friend back home who'd teased her about her climbing, and she suddenly thought; 'I'm gonna get that Polka dot jersey, and I'm gonna show that Steve Tilford that I'm a good climber'. She says, if it hadn't been for Tilford's joshing that spring, 'I don't think I would have had the guts to break away.' So she cut loose. 'I went at just my climbing speed and I got to the top with – I want to say 10 minutes and that just seems unreasonable to me – but I was really far ahead.' Having achieved her mission to net the climber's jersey, she sat up and waited for the pack. Then changed her mind and kept riding, figuring she'd get caught by an advance party at some point. But no one ever came and she rode into Grenoble alone. 'And that's when I started thinking: I could win this.' That ride also nudged her into second place on the GC, a bit over a minute behind Hage. A triumphant postcard was duly dispatched to the US.

Things started looking up. Betsy King had managed to find the team a better DS. This one couldn't speak English either, but he knew how to look after his riders. 'He was fabulous. We didn't have anything bigger than a 19 gear the first part of the race and then somehow he got us some more gears and more stuff. I don't think our new guy was official but he definitely helped us a lot. He was a totally amazing person.' Marianne also made friends with Christian Pons, a motorcycle outrider who would interpret the day's stage summaries, also known as the 'race bible', for her and tell her what was coming up.

The team, even if a little awkwardly and reluctantly, started to coalesce around its new leader.

A few days later Martin blew up the race, winning the stage into La Plagne with more than 5 minutes on Heleen Hage, and getting herself the yellow jersey, in addition to the one with the dots.

Martin remembers the exhaustion she felt on one of the Tour's rest days. 'I was sitting up in my room and I looked down on this cute little park. So I went down and sat on a park bench and then I realised I was too tired to even sit on a bench, I had to go back up and lie down. And then the next day I think I won. It's amazing what your body can do.' The stage after La Plagne, from Scionzier to Morzine, proved her most challenging test, with a climb up the 1st category Joux-Plane. The Dutch team, intent on taking back the yellow jersey, went straight on the attack. 'They'd send a rider off with Heleen on her wheel, so I had to chase them down, and then they'd send someone else off with Heleen on her wheel... and by the time we got to the big climb, I was already really tired.'

'I don't remember any of the other climbs but I remember this one, because I was tired going into it. The street was lined with people, which was so cool, but then you'd look way up and it [the summit] looks like it's 20 miles away and you can *still* see the road lined with people. And I'm like, there's *no way* I can do that. *Oh my God*. You know that feeling where you can see where you've got to go and you lose all steam because you think you can never do it?'

All she could do was take things one step at a time.

The Dutch might have had a better-organised team, but Marianne had her own secret weapon. When she'd been recovering from anaemia earlier in the spring, she'd worked with a doctor who specialised in visualisation techniques; 'it was about strength and about focus.'

'Instead of being outside and thinking, "Oh my god, look at how steep that hill is!" I went inside and felt the strength that I had.'

And so Martin stared at the tarmac in front of her wheel and simply kept repeating to herself, 'I know I can do the next 10 feet, I know I can do the next 10 feet... I cannot believe more people don't do that, because it's so powerful', Marianne says. Hage won the stage, but Marianne came second, only 22 seconds back. Enough to keep the yellow jersey, with a margin of more than 3 minutes to spare.

Mostly what she remembers is having fun, and the constant euphoria of being in the Tour, the crazy spectators on the road, parting like the waves before Moses, the chaos and the fanfare. At the end of stages, 'we'd take a bunch of USA hats out of the team car and we'd go into the crowd and we'd see somebody with a cool cycling hat and we'd go, "*Changer*? *Changer*?" We had this amazing collection of really cool cycling hats from everywhere.' In the evenings, they'd laugh about their experiences, and drink wine with their dinner.

They very rarely saw the men, who had different stage starts and therefore stayed in different towns. However at one point she recalls being taken with her teammates to one of the hotels where the men were staying. She remembers

sitting on a bench chatting to Vincent Barteau, at that point in the yellow jersey. Barteau pointed at Laurent Fignon and said, 'that man's going to win the Tour de France'.

And at that moment, Marianne found herself suddenly wanting to reply, 'And I'm going to win the women's race'. She never said the words, but she remembers to this day how they came into her head.

She remembers crossing the finish line on the Champs Elysées in Paris, still in yellow, and hearing a familiar voice shout out to her from the crowd. Her father had surprised her by coming all the way from Michigan, he had got stuck in England because of a pilot strike, but nonetheless made it to the finish on time to congratulate his prodigious, prodigal daughter.

She remembers, while waiting for the podium ceremony, meeting a reporter from one of the top US TV networks who had no idea there'd been a women's race.

She remembers going up to her hero, Jonathan Boyer, to tell him about how much he'd inspired her and him 'totally not responding. So I just walked back to my team on the other side of the room.' She remembers her friend the motorcyclist taking her round Paris the following day to see the sights. And then she remembers later that afternoon, sitting on her own in a hotel room, having, 'this huge crying spell for like 15 minutes. All this emotion that had been pent up all this time, it was just like this waterfall of emotion that came out. And then I was OK.' Then she says, 'I'm sure the guys don't do that.'

Of the 36 riders who had been at the race, 35 finished. The only one to abandon had broken her collarbone in a crash.

Martin won $1,000 dollars for winning that inaugural tour, roughly 15 times less than what Fignon would have won. Her flights to Europe, which she had had to pay for out of her own pocket, had cost her $450.

She never made any money off the back of her victory. Her federation wouldn't allow her to accept individual sponsorship, and it was too difficult to put a team together. 'This was before cell phones and long distance calls', she points out. When she retired from racing she had to work two jobs for two years to pay off all her cycling debts.

Marianne's teammate, Patty Peoples, who rode subsequent editions of the race, and still competes – and wins – duathlons now in her early 60s, has said that first women's Tour de France in 1984 was also the best, and the closest to the men's race in terms of its organisation.

Paris post-Tour party with actress Jane Seymour, men's Tour winner Laurent Fignon and his directeur sportif, Cyrille Guimard. © Denys Clement/Marianne Martin

'I love the challenge of doing something that hasn't been done before', Martin reflects. 'The Tour really taught me we can do so much more than we think we can.'

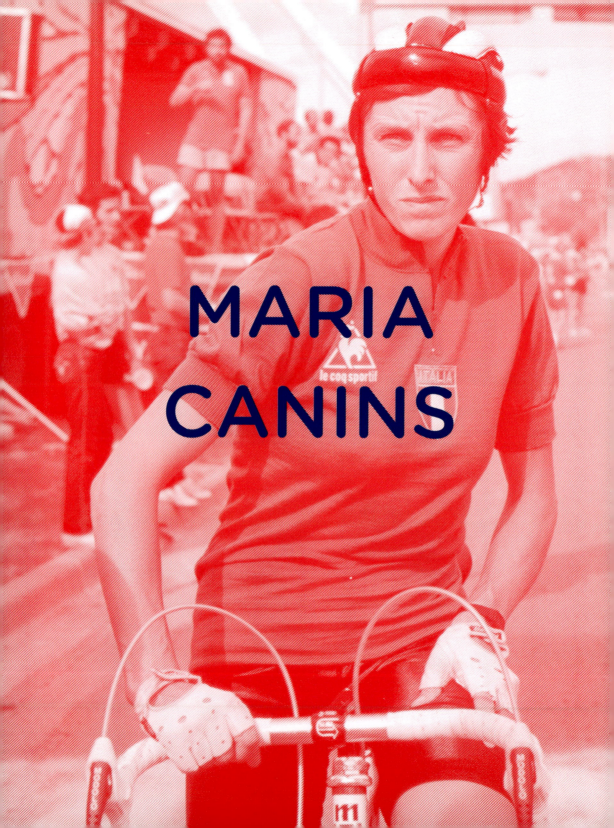

'The Flying Mother'

At an age when most riders retire, Maria Canins came out of nowhere, and won everything. She was a mother who could only train in the evenings after she'd tucked her daughter up in bed. And yet she left all the other riders standing; she would fly up the mountains while the peloton laboured and toiled down below. She had pale blue eyes with an electric intensity, and an austere, v-shaped face. With her short-cropped hair she looked like Joan of Arc, or one of those ascetic saints in a Renaissance altarpiece.

In post-race interviews she was honest and direct, the most human of riders. She was loved and feared in equal measure.

She rode – and won – her first Tour de France in 1985, when she was 36. She was the oldest rider in the peloton. She'd only been racing for three years; cycling having started out as a sideline to her brilliant cross-country skiing career.

That same year she became the first Italian to win the longest and most prestigious cross-country skiing race in the world, the *Vasaloppet*, whose 90km through the bleak Swedish winter landscape makes it one of the most physically and mentally exacting races there is. Also that year she had won the 70km *Marcialonga* – the Italian *Vasaloppet* – and the Italian national cross-country skiing championship in the 5km pursuit. In the course of her career, she won 13 national championships in cross country skiing and nine consecutive editions of the *Marcialonga*. But you can't ski all year round, so the cycling kept her busy in the summer. The results came easily and it gave her an opportunity to travel the world. Later she would say it was the sport she enjoyed the most, describing it as, 'a big game where you never know if you're to win or lose until the end.'

When the Italian cycling team had initially asked her if she'd like to have a go, she had been skiing and winning national championships for 11 years already. Two months after her initial trial road race, she came second at the worlds. By the time she lined up at the Tour de France, she was certainly one of the favourites.

There was a sense that this was the first 'real' edition of the race, since the previous year all the top riders had been at the Olympics. The second women's Tour was much more ambitious than the first, with a peloton twice the size, longer stages and more of them. As with the previous year's race, the women rode the same stages as the men, but over shorter distances, starting several hours before them. Felix Lévitan wanted the women's race to resemble the men's as closely as possible. It had seemed perfectly clear in 1984 that women were more than up to the challenge, so Lévitan's team asked the UCI to waive its ruling limiting women's stage races to only 12 days. The Tour wanted 18. The UCI refused point blank.

Lévitan refused to give in straight away. 'It is not the style of our house to throw in the towel', he said, referring to Henri Desgrange's chutzpah in the early years of the men's race. 'Since the very beginnings [of cycling] we've encountered such problems, but it takes more than this to get us to back down when our idea is good and everything shows that it is.' His two race directors, Xavier Louy and Richard Marillier, sat down with the French Cycling Federation to analyse all the rules. And then someone had the bright idea to create two races. Race A would feature a prologue and 12 stages and Race B would feature 5 stages. A day would separate the two. You couldn't do race B without doing race A, and anyone doing race A was expected to go onto B.

Since it was impossible to carry a time advance from one race to another, they decided to convert seconds into points. Jerseys also had to change colour between races, apart from the leader's jersey which remained yellow.

This second women's Tour de France was 1,150km long and featured 5 rest days. The average distances of stages lengthened, too, with flat stages averaging around 80km and mountain stages around 40km. The peloton featured 12 teams (compared to the previous year's six) and 72 riders, made up of two French teams, two American teams and individual teams from Italy, Canada, Britain, Germany, Sweden, Belgium, Holland and – the most surprising announcement of all – China.

The hot favourite was the French rider Jeannie Longo: she had already won the national championship road race, the Tour of Texas and the Coors Classic that year. Maria Canins, meanwhile, had won the Tour of Norway. Jeannie dominated the first week of the Tour, winning three stages and taking the yellow jersey. Maria, however, was nervous in hectic sprints, so she finished the flat stages in anonymity, with the sole intention of crossing the line in one piece. She fired her first warning shot in the first time trial, which she won, by two tenths of a second over Longo. Then, as the race headed into the Alps, the tables turned. Canins attacked on the Col du Corbier and simply flew away. She won the next day's stage with 8 minutes over Longo. In the Pyrenees she sailed over the Tourmalet, winning the stage again with a margin of 9 minutes. 'I thought the Tourmalet would be harder', she said later. A young American riding her first Tour, Phyllis Hines, presented a cautionary tale of what might happen if you tried to follow Maria. Phyllis was doing well, in 6th place on GC, when she tried to follow her up the Tourmalet. When Maria disappeared ahead anyway, she continued to grind on, perhaps hoping for a miracle. Under the blasting sun, she began to weave across the road and finally toppled over. She was quickly scooped up by the ambulance. Dizziness and fatigue were with her for another 48 hours. We don't need to feel too bad for Phyllis, however, since she won the Tour de l'Aude the following year, perhaps having learnt a valuable lesson in the Pyrenees.

Felix Lévitan couldn't get over it. Maria's riding called to mind the great solo efforts of her compatriots Fausto Coppi and before him Ottavio Bottechia, climbers who coolly sailed away from everyone, without apparently even breaking into a sweat. (Legend has it that Bottechia sang to himself as he climbed.) Lévitan took to calling her 'Coppi in a skirt'. The Italian press, disappointed with the performances of their riders in the men's race, were equally delighted, and started following the women's race instead. *La Gazetta dello Sport* put her on their front cover.

They called her *La Mamma Volante* – the flying mother, and would later run an interview with her, photographed at the kitchen stove. The domestic focus didn't seem to trouble her especially. It is still remarkable that she managed to juggle family life with such astounding performances. Perhaps it helped that her racing was also a family project. Her husband, who had given Maria her first racing bike, came to the Tour with his own bike and a tent. He would cycle the difficult mountain stages a day in advance, marking the roads with chalk on dangerous corners or descents. Her daughter Concetta recalls getting to sit in the team car in races.

'She always remained herself, simple and with a great sense of humility, as if she did not really understand what all the fuss was about, the magnificence of her achievements, and the effect she had on people', Concetta has written. 'Often after a race it was difficult to get close to her quickly and I had to push my way among the crowds, but my moment of triumph always came as she would lift me up high on the podium and I would dedicate a stare or two to those who had not let me pass by!'

Maria won the 1985 Tour with 22 minutes over Jeannie who came second. She would later consider it one of her best memories of racing, 'Because it was all new. Every day was a surprise. The place, the race itself, the actions. I'd never been to Paris before. I'd always watched the professionals lap the Champs-Elysées that Sunday, and I found myself there. I hadn't done cycling from an early age, I hadn't grown up in that world.' The following year Maria won the Tour again, and Jeannie was again relegated to second place in humiliating fashion, this time by 15 minutes. Inga Thompson, who came third that year, likes to point out that Maria's, 'overall winning time was only 6/10ths of a mile per

> 'Every day was a surprise. The place, the race itself, the actions.'

hour slower than Greg LeMond's average winning speed. And if you want to argue, well, the stages were shorter and the days were fewer, then I would argue our peloton was half the size. We had a little over 100 women, and the men had close to 200, so right there you could say we had half the horse power in there.' 1986 also marked Maria's last victory in the Tour. The next three years the tables turned and it was Jeannie who won and Maria who came second. Maria was still able to beat Jeannie in the *Tour de l'Aude* in 1987 and she triumphed the following year at the inaugural Women's Giro and came second the year after. However, perhaps her age was finally starting to catch up with her. She was, after all, 11 years older than Longo, and as much as twice the age of the very youngest riders.

She announced her retirement at the end of 1990 when she was 41. She was still winning, having taken the *Tour de la Drome* and the *Trofeo Alberto Binda* that season.

'I thought doping existed' she later said. 'I saw people going strong who weren't riding like that before. You can't say anything or accuse anyone, because you don't know either. It wasn't the fair, honest environment I'd felt before. I didn't want to give the satisfaction to someone passing me now, when they'd been behind before. So I stopped.' She still turned up to races, however, winning two mountain bike world championships 1991 and 1993, as well as the Trofeo Binda again in 1992. She even rode the Giro d'Italia again in 1995 when she was 46. In fact all the way up to 1999 she was taking part in amateur races in the masters category and winning them.

'Sport is your companion through life and teaches you so much', she wrote in 2014. These days she still lives in Val Badia where she is involved in the tourism industry. She still cycles and skis. If you're lucky, you might even run into her.

JEANNIE LONGO

'The Terminator'

Jeannie Longo – the first name to come to mind in the pub quiz to name a champion female cyclist. Winner of 13 World Championships (and 27 medals in total), breaker of 38 records, holder of 59 national titles, owner of four Olympic medals, one of which is gold, champion of three Tours de France, vice champion of four, vainqueur of another 40 stage races *besides* and, in total, a winner of more than 1,000 races since the beginning of her cycling career.

Then there's the length of her cycling career, with participations in seven Olympic games, her 20 national championship road race victories between 1979 and 2008. A rider unable to retire: even in 2017 she was winning her age category in the amateur world championships, and felt the need to point out that if she'd been 15 seconds faster, she would have won all the women's categories.

Jeannie Longo – a French national treasure. *La* Longo, in fact. A woman who is adored and reviled in equal measure.

'She's selfish and arrogant', said Samuel Abt, the former cycling correspondent of the *International Herald Tribune*, in 1997. 'She has antagonized officials and cost some of them their jobs. When she competed for the French team at the world championships in 1989, the other women on the team were so fed up with her behaviour that they came up with a rule: Anytime someone mentioned her name, that person had to pay a fine. Jeannie Longo is an extremely turbulent person who happens to be a very good cyclist.'

Being accused of having a terrible personality is one thing. Being involved in a doping investigation is another. In March 2017 her husband and coach, Patrice Ciprelli, was given a one-year suspended prison sentence for having illegally obtained the blood-booster EPO between 2008 and 2011. In court he declared the 33 boxes had been purchased for his personal use alone. It strains credulity to believe his wife had no idea about any of this, given their famously close collaboration. Jeannie herself has suggested in the past that Ciprelli is her Pygmalion, that she is, 'the doll he has created.'

The case now casts other minor indiscretions (which the sympathetic observer could reasonably dismiss) in a different light, such as her one-month suspension in 1987 when she tested positive for low levels of ephedrine. She claimed it hadn't been listed in a herbal supplement she had been taking and indeed *má huáng,* the plant from which ephedrine is synthesised, is commonly used in herbal teas and cold medicines. Then there is the incident in 2011 when she was accused of three 'no shows' for testing under the UCI's whereabouts programme, until it emerged that she wasn't in fact on the control list and was absolved of any wrongdoing.

She lives in a mountain chalet and keeps goats; she always eats organic; she's into aromatherapy and herbal remedies; she doesn't have a mobile phone and avoids having anything to do with computers. Systematic EPO use seems both highly plausible given her husband's role in her sports career and at the same time completely out of character.

> 'Longo is a woman who devoted her life to her sport, who cannot accept anything less than being at the very top of her game.'

So how does one consider Longo's career? With regard to the doping there are only grave doubts. And there is surely the danger of a double standard here: few are the male champions whose careers are able to stand close scrutiny on this subject. Yet many of the undoubtedly tainted remain celebrated, even lionised. It is surely absurdly reductive to attribute achievements on the scale of hers simply to doping. Longo is a woman who devoted her life to her sport, who cannot accept anything less than being at the very top of her game, who transformed and professionalised women's cycling with her fastidious attention to detail and her ability to generate media attention, draw in sponsors and attract fans.

Jeannie Longo grew up in the mountains. She was born in Annecy in 1958, the middle of three sisters. Her father was a businessman and her mother a gymnastics teacher. Her father would take her and her sisters swimming in their lunch breaks, or skiing in the mountains at weekends. Contrary to what those *Nouvelle Vague* movies might have you think, French culture is a lot about rules. To conform is to succeed. Jeannie Longo's parents didn't care too much for convention however. She went to university in Grenoble and joined the university skiing club where she met Patrice Ciprelli. Patrice was a French Olympic skier and a man obsessed with discipline and pushing everything to the limits. He became in quick succession her boyfriend and her coach. She was his project, someone he could perfect. They would go out on the slopes in all weathers, blizzards if necessary. She became French national champion in the Universities category.

She took up cycling in the summer to maintain her winter fitness, and soon people began suggesting she should have a go at racing too. Straight away, she won the French national championship in the road race in 1979, her first year of racing, a feat she would repeat for the next ten consecutive years.

For a while, the skiing and cycling overlapped. In 1979 she was also a French university champion in three different skiing disciplines. It wasn't until 1982 that she stopped competing as a skier, by which time she was already a four-time French road race champion.

In the winter Patrice had got her strength training in the gym and riding in the velodrome in Grenoble. He got her training right up at the top of the banking where you have to drive harder. She would later take part in Six-day races and win three of them, including one in Paris in 1987 in front of 10,000 spectators. She would go on to break the hour record, not just once, but six times. Immensely strong, she was a powerhouse who barrelled along the flat and could win sprints from 800 metres out. And while it wasn't her forte, she could hold her own in the mountains, too.

But many of her biggest objectives were plagued with bad luck. The 1980 world championships, held near her parents in Sallanches, were a disaster, with the team setting off late and the bus arriving only 15 minutes before the race started. Her dreams of an Olympic medal at the 1984 Olympics were dashed in the final 500 metres, when Maria Canins' pedal got caught in her derailleur. In 1998 she broke her femur a month before the Olympics, but still went to the race, finishing 21st. In 1992 she didn't realise the Australian rider Kathryn Watt had already gone up the road, crossing the line in second place, thinking that she'd won.

She calls herself an 'authentic pessimist'. Rémy Pigois, the former speaker of the women's Tour de France, wrote about her fragile morale, which was 'not at all on a par with her exceptional physical qualities.' In addition to falling out with teammates and antagonising the French Cycling Federation, she would have fearsome bust-ups with her husband. 'I'll admit it, I have a difficult character', she writes in her autobiography. 'I'm very uncompromising. It's not a bad thing. You can be difficult and very nice at the same time.'

In 1985 Jeannie had an opportunity to get her 'revenge' on Maria Canins and Olympic failure when both riders represented their countries at the second ever women's Tour de France. Jeannie won five flat stages, Maria won five in the mountains. Jeannie took home the green sprinters' jersey. Maria took home the yellow and polka dot jerseys. No one, but no one, could hold on to Maria up there in the mountains. It drove Jeannie mad.

At the chaotic podium presentation in Paris, in front of Bernard Hinault, all swagger at having dominated yet again, the different jersey winners of the women's race trudged out on the stage, looking like awkward children. Jeannie in green looked like thunder, like she'd lost. Winning the sprinters jersey and coming second overall counted for nothing.

But by the end of the summer she got her revenge, winning the world championships in Italy on Maria's home turf. The victory was all the sweeter in that it was a hilly course, and she had managed to stick with Maria on all the climbs. She had no qualms about hanging on to other riders' wheels if necessary: there's only one reason for being in a race, and if you're not doing everything you can to win it, then you might as well go home. It was the first of four consecutive world championship victories in the road race, a feat no rider – male or female – has equalled.

Jeannie suffered another humiliating defeat to Maria in the 1986 Tour de France, but the following year the tables turned. She had broken the hour record for the first time at the end of the season which no doubt buoyed her, and in the spring of 1987 she went to Colombia to race – and win – the Tour of Colombia, as much for the high-altitude training as for the race itself. She had lost weight, and with it some of her powerful sprint, but in exchange she had become a better climber. It was a gamble she was willing to take if it gave her a chance of winning the Tour.

It was a very close race: despite winning the prologue, she failed to win sprints in the first week that she might previously have mastered. She berated her team for failing to chase down the Dutch rider Monique Knol who took the yellow jersey. But when the race went up Luz Ardiden, the first of the mountains, she was not only able to stick with Maria, but leave her a minute behind by the summit.

Canins took back 30 seconds in a time trial the following day, and then they duelled their way in thrilling fashion across the Alps. It was finally on the Joux Plane on the last mountain stage that Jeannie won the Tour, putting 3 minutes into Maria.

Jeannie's sudden improvements were so dramatic that a number of riders were taken aback, including Canins. 'How did she do it? I've always asked myself that too', she said in an interview in 2017. 'Because I didn't get any worse. I was doing the Passo Campolongo and the Passo Valparola in training, and my times were the same as the previous year.' Inga Thompson, who had come third in 1986, was also struck by the change. 'I had been racing against Jeannie Longo for a few years already. She was always cutting-edge – she always had the lightest bikes and the latest equipment, and she was consistently a strong competitor', she said in an interview in 2014. 'Even though she was really good in the road races, I could out-climb her in any race. In the time trials, I could take a few seconds, maybe up to a minute out of her each time. But in the spring of 1987, suddenly Jeannie just completely exploded. We were at the Tour of Texas, I was putting my usual time gaps on Jeannie through the road stages, but when I went to Europe six weeks later, Jeannie was putting two and three minute improvements into me in the time trials, even when I was still putting a minute or more into everyone else!' Seasoned followers of cycling know the implications of these comments. But it's important to note that 1987 would be extremely early for the use of the synthetic red blood cell stimulating hormone EPO, which had only just come out of clinical trials in 1986. It is not thought to have entered the male peloton until the end of the 1980s, more probably the beginning of the 1990s. Blood doping? The simple logistics of storing, transporting and administering blood throughout a busy season without a powerful team or political interests facilitating things makes that seem doubtful. Can we accept that weight loss and high-altitude training could have made all the difference? Maybe. The transformative effect of carrying less weight when riding up mountains is elementary physics and altitude training prompts the body to produce more red blood cells in a natural equivalent to EPO use. Nevertheless unease remains.

1987 marked the first of a three-year reign over the Tour for Longo. Those were the glory years of her career, when she seemed to win everything she tried her hand at. Her palmarès in this period is staggering. Take 1987 alone, perhaps her most impressive year, in which she was world champion and French national champion, in which she won eight stages and the general classification of the Tour of Colombia, five stages and the GC of the Tour de la Drôme, four stages and the GC of the Tour of Norway, three stages and the GC of the Tour de France, four stages and the GC of the Coors Classic, two stages and third place overall of the Tour de l'Aude, and in which she won the Critérium des As, the Texas Cup and the Chrono des Herbiers, a major time trial. She also won the Six-day races in Paris and Grenoble and set a new hour record of 44.933km in Colorado Springs. Most riders would devote their whole career trying to get just one of those results on their palmarès. You wonder how she even managed to fit all these races onto her calendar, let alone win them.

> 'Jeannie had hit the big time, as much a household name in France as the top male athletes.'

That year a Texan friend helped her get one of the most powerful sports agents in America, who was opening an office in Paris. The agent knew nothing about cycling but everything about sponsorship and money. Suddenly Longo had a team, with sponsors who paid all the riders a salary. It was the first of its kind in France.

Jeannie had hit the big time, as much a household name in France as the top male athletes. She received lucrative contracts to take part in post Tour criterium races – normally only organised for the men's Tour winners. The honours started rolling in too: she was invited to Vienna, Barcelona, Madrid, Brussels, Cannes and Monaco to receive awards. She rubbed shoulders with Diego Maradona, Pelé, Mark Spitz. She received a Légion d'Honneur, met French President Chirac, the Colombian President, Prince Albert of Monaco. She was put up in five-star hotels.

Longo did something no other French rider had done before: bring women's cycling into the spotlight, and it wouldn't have happened if she hadn't won the women's Tour de France. It was something she had understood all along: as far as the general public was concerned, only the Tour and the Olympics mattered.

But there were other ambitions too, outside sport. In 1989 she stepped away from it all. She was 31 and wanted to start a family. Her doctor suggested she give the bike a break and put on a bit of weight. She took on a job with a regional sports committee coaching women and children, and helped organise the first French national championships for juniors. But she was plagued with the same career versus motherhood doubts that so many other women have had to struggle with, and the desire to do things 'right'. Could she be a mother and also race at the top level? Would she lose her edge as a rider? Would she get drawn back into the sport and not be able to enjoy her baby's infancy? In her autobiography she confesses; 'I was worried about not being able to assume my role of mother insofar as I thought Patrice would push me back into competing. And, in the end, the child wasn't enough of a two-person project.'

With Patrice Ciprelli. 1992 Barcelona Olympics. She was second in the road race. © Presse Sports/Offside

Jeannie en route to winning the 1989 world's road race. © Presse Sports/Offside

She returned to racing in 1991 with the intention of having a shot at the 1992 Barcelona Olympics. Things got off to a rocky start with French Cycling Federation when they took her off the team for the 1991 world championships.

Her crime was refusing to ride with the pedals provided by their sponsor, which she didn't get on with. She took the federation to court over the winter, and won her case, but the experience shook her.

She was anxious and depressed at the Olympics and flunked her chances of a medal in the pursuit. She came second in the road race. She carried on racing, picking up other victories along the way. Patrice took care of her training plans, ordered the bikes and the parts, and contact with Federation was made only when strictly necessary.

In 1994 she was banned from the Federation after chasing down a break containing two of her teammates at the world championships in Sicily. In her autobiography she points out that nobody was on her wheel when she did this and that she hadn't brought the peloton with her. By 1996 while the French riders were all attending a training camp in Atlanta prior to the Olympics, Jeannie was on her own in the mountains of Colorado. She always felt at home in America. She liked the razzamatazz of American women's races, the fact that American champions could concentrate on being the best, without having to apologise for it. In 1997 she even toyed with the idea of changing nationality.

America rewarded her affection and she finally won her gold medal in Atlanta, riding the final 11km to the finish on her own. For a moment, before crossing the line, her face had a look of haunted exhaustion beyond her 38 years. Then she looked up, turned around as if she couldn't quite believe there hadn't been another mistake, another unaccounted for rider sneaking up on her, and finally a smile flooded her features, expressing relief as much as joy.

Like Beryl Burton, Jeannie was unable to walk away from the sport when she was at her peak, and like Burton, she ended up being bitterly resented by the younger generation of riders who felt she stood in their way. When she failed to get selected for the 2012 Olympics she admitted to having 'black thoughts' and in the same breath declared she understood why some athletes become suicidal at the end of their careers.

> 'I am sad. I am unwanted. I'm resented for being here'

'I am sad. I am unwanted. I'm resented for being here', she told *l'Equipe*. 'In other sports, you say goodbye to athletes like me with a little tear in the eye and a bit of ceremony. That's not really what I'm asking for, but at least just a little bit of recognition.'

'She was like a meteorite passing, which had its moment but which didn't really serve women's cycling as it might have done', says Josette Leulliot, who met Longo on many occasions, not least when Jeannie won five editions of the *Trophée des Grimpeurs* race that Josette organised. Josette is the daughter of Jean Leulliot who created the first women's Tour de France in 1955, and who reinstated *Paris-Nice* in 1951. She inherited the latter when he died in 1982 and consequently became the first female race organiser in France. 'She inspired young riders, that's for sure', says Leulliot, but could she have done more? 'It's such a shame that in her moment of glory, when she had everything, that she didn't do more to break the barriers because she was the greatest, she had everything. But I don't know if you can be such a great champion and still have a mind or the time to spare to improve things for those who follow.' Leulliot points out that Jeannie achieved everything in isolation, with Patrice's support of course, but never with the Federation's backing.

'She really fought, all on her own, to get to where she got. I think at some point she thought, I don't give a damn, I'm racing for myself. I've had to do everything myself, so can everyone else.'

Who is Jeannie Longo? 'Not for one moment have I considered myself lucky', she told *l'Equipe* after she narrowly avoided a fatal helicopter accident in 2015 that killed ten people, including three top French athletes. 'When it really comes down to it, it would have been better if I had replaced one of the young ones because Camille Muffat was only 25.'

Longo has battled everyone and everything: records, mountains, sexism, her federation, self-doubt, rivals, officials and ageism. It's the latter that finally made her a popular heroine, the way in which she carried on winning races against girls old enough to be her daughter.

Why should she have 'stepped aside' for younger riders if she was still capable of winning races? And why should she be obliged to be sweet natured and charming about it too? Why should female athletes be reviled when they exhibit the same single-minded ruthlessness that is revered in their male counterparts? Why should Eddy Merckx be mythologised for his determination to win every race, why should he be absolved for his many drug busts, while Longo be shunned for her assumed but unproven cheating?

For now, no one believes in Jeannie Longo. And that's the tragedy of her story.

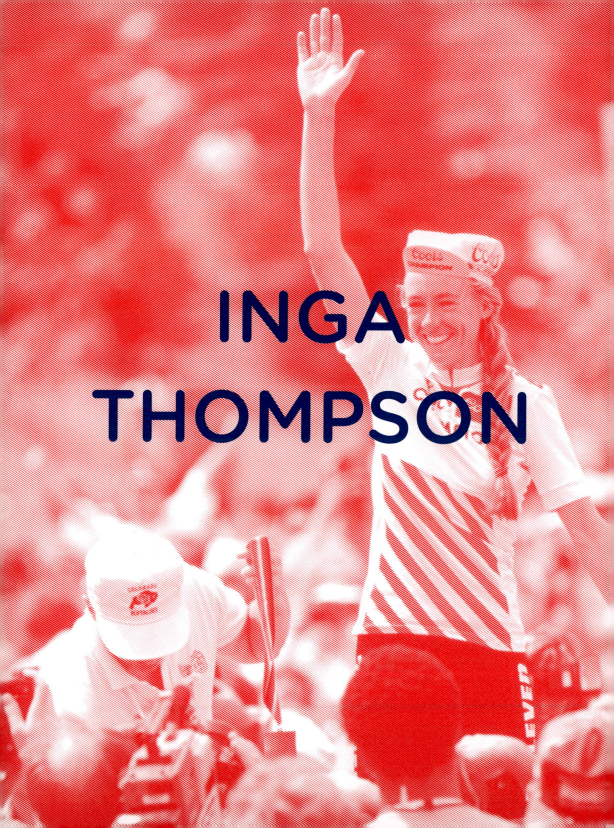

'Helga'

'I remember them talking about how they're going to have the first women's Tour de France. And the first ever women's Olympics. That's what got me riding on a bike. There were all these great races for women', says Inga Thompson.

Inga Thompson's cycling career coincided with a brief, golden and largely forgotten age of women's stage racing. While she was somewhat overshadowed by Jeannie Longo and Maria Canins - she twice came third in the Tour de France while they battled it out for first and second – Inga was the other, great stage racer of the late 1980s and early 1990s. She may not have won the Tour, but she won something even tougher: the 17 stage Ore-Ida Women's Challenge. 'The UCI would not approve it because they thought it was too extreme, and that became their (the race organiser's) motto that year; let's get extreme. We had a 125 mile stage in one of those stages.' The race, which took place in Idaho, featured amongst other things Galena Summit, which at 8,701 feet (2,652m) above sea level is the highest road mountain pass in the Northwest.

That race was the vision of Jim Rabdau, a former Green Beret with a 25-year career in the military, who had served in Vietnam and had been a platoon leader in a parachute regiment. He had first encountered bike racing while posted in Italy, when the car that he was driving was held up at a cross roads so a peloton could pass. He was instantly drawn to the spectacle of it all. As you might imagine, Rabdau's race was planned with military precision, something the riders, in an era of low-budget, ad-hoc race organisation, greatly appreciated.

'After 17 days, the staff was tired', he later said. 'The girls (racers) were just getting into it.'

At its peak, the race had a prize fund of $125,000 – the biggest of any cycling race whether for men or women, in America.

Not having a cycling background meant Rabdau paid no heed to established ideas on how to run races. So in addition to making the race long and hard, he made it open to everyone, amateurs and professionals alike. 'That's where Rabdau was really great, he was like, put together a team, you get to go', says Inga. 'It was really cool. There were several little ragtag teams in there and you know? They stuck it out. It was awesome.' Rabdau later said; 'I've always thought in my life, that if you can be around people who are excellent, then you'll know what excellence is. That was a lot of what I was trying to do – to get girls to that level'.

Mixed in with the primarily American, Canadian and Australian riders was a Lithuanian team that came every year. Their coach once turned up with two suitcases; one contained vodka and caviar, the other spare parts and underwear.

Inga Thompson was one of those prodigiously talented riders who seemed to come out of nowhere and just excel, right from the very start. She had been a competitive runner, on the back of which she had secured a scholarship to the California Polytechnical University at San Luis Obispo to study engineering. A recurring ankle injury prompted her to take up cycling instead. Straight away, at the age of 20, she won the first three races she ever took part in.

Her fourth race was an Olympic qualifier event, and then the Olympic trials road race. She made it onto the Olympic team and Connie Carpenter-Phinney invited her to ride with her road team to get some experience. 'I remember we did a criterium in New York; it was the first one I'd ever done and I didn't understand the tactics at all. I suffered like a dog! It was a humbling day, but I was learning quickly.' Thompson became a popular rider who was easy to spot in races with her distinctively long Rapunzel hair tied in a plat and pinned to her jersey. Tough racing was exactly what Inga liked. Like most of the women interviewed for this book, she would have preferred longer races, and found the maximum distances of 50 miles, or 80km, that were prescribed at the time by the UCI, to be 'ridiculous. When you're a racer, you're not even warmed up at 50 miles... [that's] when the racing really starts happening.'

It's tempting to contrast the UCI's kid glove approach to women's racing with Henri Desgrange's notorious fantasy, entertained in the early years of the Tour de France, of creating a race that was so difficult, only one rider would make it back to Paris.

A good stage race like the Ore-Ida was 'meant to be hard', says Inga, 'it wasn't meant to be easy enough that everyone could finish. That's why we're there. We're not parading! We're racing!' Inga remembers a stage in the now defunct Tour de la Drôme as one of her greatest rides. The race took place in the Alps in 1988 at the same time Andy Hampsten famously won the Giro d'Italia in a blizzard.

'We were in that same storm', says Inga. 'We did two mountain passes and of course nobody had checked about the weather. I had sent ahead some cold weather clothes in our follow vehicle. I remember I was in a skin suit. I think it was a 50 mile or 80km race: it was a long race. It started to rain, and then it started to slush, and then it started to snow. And then the next thing you know we're in this full-on slush storm and my hands are frozen to the bars and my derailleur's trying to freeze up and we came down this pass.' At this point, after making repeated requests for her jacket, Inga learnt from her Directeur Sportif that all the clothes had in fact been sent on ahead to the stage finish. 'I remember just looking down this pass we had to descend, and thinking, "we just came up this climb and I am so cold, and now I gotta go down that!" And then I outsprinted Longo at the finish and won.' After the race, Inga was shaking so violently from cold she had to ask her DS to pre-chew her energy bar for her. 'Andy Hampsten walked out of [the Giro] with I don't know how many hundreds and thousands of dollars, and I won a pepper grinder!' It's hard to believe now how many great stage races there were for women during this period. Off the top of her head Inga lists the Postgiro (a tour of Norway), the Tour de l'Aude, the Tour de la Drôme, the Tour de France, the Coors Classic and the Bisbee, 'which was a hard five- or six-day race'.

Those were just a handful of the top races. Going through albums from the period and other contemporary sources, I've managed to find about 30 stage races launched between 1973 and 1990, almost all of which have since disappeared.

The lack of records is a problem that affects all defunct races from the pre-digital era. It's left to riders like Inga to tell their tales, and to yellowing clippings in scrapbooks to know what actually happened.

Inga illustrates the problem when she mentions she'd been looking at the list of results for the US women's national championships. 'It was like, *hey! I* won those nationals *here* and *here*, and it didn't even go back that far. And one of them wasn't right – *we won that year!* – and they had a reserve team winning. How do you correct *that* one, 25 years later?' The same goes for Inga's palmarès. Any stories that have been written about her in recent years have evidently been based on her Wikipedia page, but whoever has compiled it has missed quite a few important results. 'There are a lot of races that aren't on there', she acknowledges. 'Bisbee, I won that multiple years in a row and it was a big women's stage race. And it's not even listed on there. And I won tons of stages in the Coors Classic and that's not listed. And now I'm sitting here thinking, where do I even go and *find* that information?'

'I came across this newspaper article, and it shows me winning the race!' she says laughing. 'I don't even remember being there! It just shows you how many races we had.' Even more undocumented is the history of women taking part in men's races in the US, not because they hoped to win, but because they found the higher speeds and more aggressive racing styles beneficial for their training. 'It was all I could do to finish these things, but I still finished in the middle of the field', Thompson recalls.

> **'Andy Hampsten walked out of [the Giro] with I don't know how many hundreds and thousands of dollars, and I won a pepper grinder!'**

She recalls being in a local race called the Washington Trust which featured Alexi Grewal, the 1984 Olympic champion. Inga had hopped on to the wheel of Alexi's teammate who was trying to bridge a gap, which wound up Grewal, 'because he thought that I had chased down his teammate', she recalls. 'I had Alexi Grewal screaming at me that women shouldn't be on a bike and that I shouldn't be there', she recounts, 'and I said that I had my category pro 1:2 licence as well, I had the right to be there'. As they continued to race, the

argument went back and forth, with Inga saying, 'if I can't be here, then how come they let me in?'

Another time Inga rode a very good uphill prologue. Afterwards a professional rider came up to her and said, 'I used to tell everyone I was going to quit the first woman who beat me. But it was you and that doesn't count'. Another stage of the Washington Trust race featured a 'super hard circuit', with, 'this wall you had to climb with a long gradual uphill and a screaming downhill and I was up trying to bridge up to gaps and breaks'. Afterwards the same rider came up to Inga, 'and he just said, you have earned my respect, as far as hanging in there with the men, and not just hanging in but making attacks and trying to make moves.'

Thompson believes the gap in abilities between male and female riders at elite level is not the great gulf that we generally assume to be the case. She says the men's races were 'quite similar in the sense of the speed and intensity, it was just the races were longer and there was more depth', by which she means a larger peloton. However, she remembers the women's international races being very hard, too.

'I'm not going to say it was just as hard, but it *was* hard. The only difference being that I could make more decisive moves and every once in a while get away. But it wasn't very often that I rode off the front and there were also times with the men where I almost got away.'

'I don't want to say what comes first, the chicken or the egg,' she concludes, 'To me it's very clear: you have to have the races... The women will turn up and they will want to race. Build it and they will come.'

Notes on sources:

This book owes an enormous debt to the many riders and their descendants who generously gave me their time. I am immensely grateful to them for sharing their fascinating, moving and entertaining stories with me. I have been equally reliant on the work of cycling historians and enthusiasts who have committed so much time and research to celebrating these women. In roughly the order of the chapters with which they helped, I would especially like to thank: Alice Olson Roepke, Roger Gilles, Denis Sarazin-Charpentier, Roy Mize, Dries De Zaeytijd, Michael Townsend, Ken Mansell, George Nelson, Rod Charles, Ray Bowles, Jim Fitzpatrick, Iris Dixon, Dawn Trowell, Dr. William Wilson, Peter Whitfield, Jan Heine, Lyli Herse (RIP), Danielle Crueize, Mike, Michael and Dede Barry, Jim Cottier, Martin Hall, Jean Slack, Roger and Kevin Christian, Yvonne Reynders, Jos Vekemans, Maurice Hermans, Herbie Sykes, Denise Burton-Cole, Bernadette Malvern, Marina Kotchetova, Katya Hera, Sergey Gusev, Nikolai Razouvaev, Sandra Wright Sutherland, Keetie van Oosten-Hage, Bella Hage, Susan Noome, Marianne Martin, Josette Leulliot and Inga Thompson.

Principal sources include:

Books:

Women on the Move: The Forgotten Era of Women's Bicycle Racing, Roger Gilles, 2018
Si 1900 M'était Conte... Les Femmes à Bicyclette à la Belle Epoque, Claude Pasteur, 1986
Cycling and Society, edited by Dave Horton, Paul Rosen, Peter Cox, chapter 2: *Capitalising on Curiosity: Women's Professional Cycle Racing in the Late-Nineteenth Century,* Clare S. Simpson, 2007
Gli anni ruggenti di Alfonsina Strada. Il romanzo dell'unica donna che ha corso il giro d'Italia assieme agli uomini, Paolo Facchinetti, 2004
A Whirr of Many Wheels - Cycling in Geelong (A Chronicle from 1914 to 1945), Volume Two, Rod Charles, 2015
Wheeling Mathilda: The Story of Australian Cycling, Jim Fitzpatrick, 2013
Marguerite Wilson: The First Star of Women's Cycling, produced and edited by Dr William Wilson MB BS DCH, 2014
Cycling Cultures, edited by Peter Cox, chapter 8: *Women, gendered roles, domesticity and cycling in Britain, 1930-1980*, Peter Cox, 2015
12 Champions, Peter Whitfield, 2007
One More Kilometre and We're in the Showers: Memoirs of a Cyclist, Tim Hilton, 2004
René Herse: The Bikes, The Builder, The Riders, Jan Heine, 2012
Yvonne Reynders: Zeven Maal de Zevende Hemel, Maurice Hermans
Chasing the Rainbow: The Story of Road Cycling's World Championships, Giles Belbin, 2017
NO BRAKES! Bicycle Track Racing in the United States, Sandra Wright Sutherland, 1996
Elsy Jacobs: "Grande-Duchesse" de la Petite Reine, Gaston Zangerlé, 2000
Personal Best: The Autobiography of Beryl Burton, Beryl Burton, 1986, re-printed 2009
Ledi Lubov ILI I Eto Vse O Ney (Леди Любовь ИЛИ И это все о ней), Marina Kotchetova, Grif and Co, 2009
Rainbow Quest: The Adventurous Life of Audrey McElmury, America's First World Road Cycling Champion, Sandra Wright Sutherland, 2016
Ride the Revolution: The Inside Stories from Women in Cycling, edited by Suze Clemitson, chapter 5: *From Silver Blades to Golden Bikes,* Connie Carpenter-Phinney, 2015
Hearts of Lions: The History of American Bicycle Racing, Peter Nye, 1988
Les Petites Reines du Tour de France, Rémy Pigois, 1986
Jeannie par Longo, Jeannie Longo, 2010

Newspaper archives:

Trove.nla.gov.au (Australia)
Newspapers.com (U.S.A)
Britishnewspaperarchive.co.uk (Great Britain) Gallica.bnf.fr (France) Zefys.staatsbibliothek-berlin.de (Germany)

Deceased riders' archives:

Tillie Anderson archive, held by her great niece, Alice Olson Roepke
Doreen Middleton archive, Dawn Trowell Collection, Cycling Victoria History Archive
Marguerite Wilson archive, held by Dr William Wilson
Millie Robinson archive, held by her nephew, Kevin Christian
René Herse family and business archives, René Herse cycles
Audrey McElmury archive, held by Sandra Wright Sutherland and Michael Levonas

Also:

Beryl Burton, Summer Sport Special, Yorkshire Television, 1986, Roger Greenwood.

The following articles have also been particularly helpful:

Tillie Anderson, The Terrible Swede, by Heather Drieth, in The Wheelmen, 2000
Evelyn Hamilton – Cyclist and Heroine? Michael Townsend, classiclightweights.co.uk, 2011
Eileen Sheridan, "This Girl Can", Jack Thurston, Rouleur, issue 33
Following "Les Girls" for 400km in Normandy, Jock Wadley, Coureur, 1955
Millie Robinson, Woman of the Hour! Jock Wadley, Coureur, 1958
The Grand Duchess, Herbie Sykes, Procycling, issue 197
The Grand Prix des Nations has an Unexpected Star, Jock Wadley, International Cycle Sport, 1968
Maria Canins: Queen of the Mountains, Andy McGrath, Rouleur
The High Priest of American Road Racing – A Talk with Michael Aisner: Part 1, Steve Maxwell and Joe Harris, The Outer Line, 2017
Rabdau Reflects on the Women's Challenge, Marti Stephen, VeloNews.com, 2008
Perspectives on Doping in Pro Cycling – 2: Inga Thompson, Joe Harris and Steve Maxwell, The Outer Line, 2014
Diabolique, Dana Thomas, Outside Magazine, May 1997

Websites and blogs:
sheilahanlon.com, thevictoriancyclist.wordpress.com, historicwings.com, sixday.org.uk, rra.org.uk (the UK's Road Records Association website) ttlegends.org, memoire-du-cyclisme.eu, bikeraceinfo.com, lepetitbraquet.fr, velonews.com, Velofeminin.over-blog.com, britishpathe.com, ina.fr

Image credits:

Covers
Front: Marguerite Wilson
© Beverley Aldeslade Collection
Back: Connie Carpenter-Phinney
© Peter Read Miller/Sports Illustrated Getty Images

Front: Yvonne Reynders
© Ron Kroon/Anefo/DNA
Back: Evelyn Hamilton
© Micky Bannon

Front: Yvonne Reynders
© Ron Kroon/Anefo/DNA
Back: Marianne Martin
© Denys Clement/Marianne Martin

Endpaper front DPS – Marianne Martin and co. On the Avenue des Champs-Élysées. © Denys Clement/Marianne Martin

Endpaper front facing – Galina Ermolaeva, individual sprint world champion. © Sputnik/Topfoto

Endpaper rear facing – Marguerite Wilson's London to York ride. Jock Wadley hands up a sponge. © Beverley Alderslade Collection

Endpaper rear DPS – Yvonne Reynders celebrating. © Yvonne Reynders Collection

Contents – Beryl Burton pursuit bronze at the 1971 worlds. © Popperfoto/Getty

24 – Hélène Dutrieux promoting Dunlop tyres on a Simpson Lever Chain bicycle. © BtA

29 – By 1911, Hélène set numerous flying records including winning Italy's Coppa del Rei trophy, against the men. Library of Congress Washington DC

33 – Hélène did many crazy bike stunts. Once missing the landing and saving herself by grabbing onto a rope with one hand. © La Vie Au Grand Air/BtA

34 – Alfonsina carried postcard portraits, like this one, which she gave to roadside fans at the Giro. © akg-images/Interfoto/Friedrich

42 – Setting off from London to John o' Groats in 1935 with Labour leader Ben Tillett (L) and Claud Butler (R). © Micky Bannon

45 – Evelyn off to ride 1,000 miles in 7 days in 1934. © JA Hampton/Topical Press/Getty

46 – And she's back... © Micky Bannon

49 – Who needs a car when you have a bike and a trailer? © Gamma Keystone/Getty

52 – Marguerite catches up on the news on the way back from breaking the Land's End-John o' Groats record. © Beverley Aldeslade Collection

59 – Tea break. Sticklepath village, Devon. En route to John o' Groats. © Beverley Aldeslade Collection

62 – Plotting routes. © William Wilson collection

63 – With Dutch sprinter, Arie Van Vliet, Wembley track, 1939. © Beverley Aldeslade Collection

66 – Billie Samuel and koala bear mascot, Sydney to Melbourne. State Library of New South Wales

73 – Lunch during Valda Unthank's seven day continuous record. With Ossie Nicholson (to her left), Jack O'Donohue and Mrs M Smith (R). State Library Victoria

77 – Valda Unthank and Hubert Opperman pose for Peters Ice Cream. 1939 State Library Victoria

82 – Eileen and friends in the garage gym her husband set up.
© Eileen Sheridan

82 – A sponsor's dream.
© Eileen Sheridan

87 – Eileen during Land's End to John o' Groats. © Eileen Sheridan

89 – Sheridan spread an infectious joy to her fans. © Eileen Sheridan

93 – After the London to Portsmouth and back record, 1952. © John Chillingworth/Picture Post/Getty

94 – In the race leader's white jersey. 1955 Women's Tour de France.
© Presse Sports/Offside

99 – Lyli led the first women's Tour de France until just before the final time trial. © Presse Sports/Offside

103 – Lyli's father holds her bike, her mother looks on from behind.
© René Herse Archive

104 – René André and Lyli at a cyclocross in the snow, 1945. René Herse holding the tandem.
© René Herse Archive

106 – Winning on a chrome plated René Herse. © René Herse Archive

108 – Millie takes the weekend off work to break the hour record in Milan. © Kevin Christian Collection

113 – Breaking the hour record in Milan, with mentor Reg Harris.
© Kevin Christian Collection

119 – Ambitious and determined, yet Millie rarely talked about her achievements. © Kevin Christian Collection

120 – The first ever women's world champion, in 1958. © Presse Sports/Offside

124 – At the 1955 women's Tour de France. © Presse Sports/Offside

125 – Elsy (L), Lyli Herse (M) and Millie Robinson (R) the stars of 1950s racing. © Presse Sports/Offside

128 – Beryl Burton teaches her daughter Denise how to ride a bike.
© John Pratt/Keystone/Getty

132 – Beryl and Charlie Burton.
© Bernard Thompson

139 – Bronze ride at the 1970 worlds, behind Russians Garkushina and Obodovskaya. © Nevill Chadwick/Keystone/Getty

142 – Yvonne Reynders, Amsterdam 1967. © Ron Kroon/Anefo/Dutch National Archives

154 – Lubow Kochetova at the start of a pursuit, 1960. © Sputnik/Topfoto

159 – 1967 world road race podium (L-R) Lyubov Zadorozhnaya, Beryl Burton and Anna Konkina.
© Jac. de Nijs/Anefo/Dutch National Archives

160 (L) – Tamara Garkushina, unbeatable six-time world champion in the 3000m pursuit.
© Sputnik/TopFoto.co.uk

160 (R) and 161 – Sprinter Galina Ermolaeva won six world championships between 1958 and 1972. (middle) © Sputnik/TopFoto.co.uk (right) © Sputnik/TopFoto.co.uk

167 – Maria Lukshina, Tamara Novikova, Valentina Yurkina and Vera Gorbatcheva lead the chase, 1958 worlds. Novikova and Lukshina finished 2nd and 3rd. © Presse Sports/Offside

170 – The original Alpha girl of American cycling. © Audrey Elmury Collection

175 – The only woman in a Marine Depot race in San Diego. © Audrey Elmury Collection

178 – Preparing to destroy a pursuit opponent. © Norman/Elizabeth Bruns

179 – A moment of reflection.
© Audrey Elmury Collection

180 – Keetie (L) and Bella on a long club ride before they started racing.
© Bella Hage

185 – Keetie wins 3000m pursuit gold, 1979 world championships. Teammate Anne Möhlmann-Riemersma was second. © Rob Bogaerts/Anefo/Dutch National Archive

189 – Bella (L) and Keetie. The first women allowed to train on the Amsterdam velodrome. © Bella Hage

190 – Celebrating at the 1982 Coors Classic with teammates (L-R) Rebecca Daughton, Marianne Berglund and Sue Novara-Reber. © Brian Brainerd/Denver Post/Getty

195 – 1984 Olympic road race with, from left: Rebecca Twigg, Connie and Kristin Thompson. © Steve Powell/Getty

200 – Marianne Martin riding into yellow at the 1984 Tour at La Plagne.
© Denys Clement/Marianne Martin

203 – Team Etats Unis wait in the shade for the start. © Denys Clement/Marianne Martin

208 – Translating the day's route.
© Denys Clement/Marianne Martin

209 – A Perrier after the race, in time honoured Tour de France tradition.
© Denys Clement/Marianne Martin

212 – Maria representing Italy at the 1984 Coors Classic, which she won.
© Beth Schneider

217 – At Morzine, 1985 Tour de France. Longo, on Maria's wheel, lost the yellow jersey by the stage end. © Presse Sports/Offside

220 – Longo wins the 3000m pursuit world championships. Grenoble 1986.
© Gerard Malie/AFP/Getty

230 – Inga Thompson wins the 1988 Coors Classic. © Beth Schneider

235 – Inga and her plat on the podium at the 1985 Coors Classic. © Beth Schneider

237 – 1986 Coors Classic. After dropping Longo on the final climb.
© Duane Howell/Denver Post/Getty

Acknowledgements:

I would like to thank the folks at Rapha first and foremost for having the vision to publish this book. Queens of Pain owes its existence to Taz Darling and Guy Andrews and their immense commitment to the project. David Luxton and Rebecca Wilson got me to the start line and the very talented Melanie Mues, Jo Walton and Anya Hayes have been quite the 'A' team, all the way to the finish. I'd like to thank my parents for all their constant support and Leonie, Penelope and Mathilda for being such champions. Most importantly I would like to thank Jonathan: my own Charlie, Ken and Carlo. I couldn't have written this without your help.
–Isabel Best

Editor's thanks:

Once again we're indebted to all of our 'rebel stars' of production; Melanie Mues, Anya Hayes, Jo Walton, Linda Duong and Kate Keown. Many thanks to all those who helped with images, especially; Peter Whitfield, Jack Thurston, Marianne Martin and Beth Schneider. Thanks to the photo agency gang; Saad Javed and Stephen Kirkby at Getty Images and Charlotte Wilson at Offside. I also need to mention Manuel Lozano, Vi Hernando and Kitty from the Wan ke Long concept store, who know you either rock, or you suck. Thanks to all Rapha Queens; Emma Wallace, Sarah Clark, Marta Gut, Alicia Bamford, Kati Jagger and Amy Whitling for all their energy and enthusiasm. Lastly to all the 'Queens of Pain' and to Isabel for telling their amazing stories so well, we hope they inspire some future legends.
–Taz Darling